*The Institutional Nature
of Adult Christian Education*

The
Institutional Nature
of
Adult Christian
Education

by
BRUCE REINHART

Philadelphia
THE WESTMINSTER PRESS

CE
268.434
R275

COPYRIGHT © MCMLXII W. L. JENKINS

All rights reserved—no part of this book may be reproduced in any form without permission in writing from the publisher, except by a reviewer who wishes to quote brief passages in connection with a review in magazine or newspaper.

158753

LIBRARY OF CONGRESS CATALOG CARD NO. 62–9809

To

Suzanne and Holly

PRINTED IN THE UNITED STATES OF AMERICA

CONTENTS

INTRODUCTION

As THIS WRITER BEGAN a concentrated professional interest in the field of adult education in the church, a basic question was frequently asked by colleagues in the ministry, namely: "What part does adult education play in the life of the church?" A closely related question was frequently asked by adult educators in other fields: "What role will the church play in the emerging adult education movement?"

As answers to these questions were sought, numerous frustrations arose. Foremost among them was the apparent discrepancy between the theological rationale for adult education in the church which tended to emphasize what *ought* to be, rather than what *actually* existed. A vigorous theological interest in the educational functions of the church by educators invariably placed education at the heart of the religious enterprise. What Christian educators have been saying may well be summed up in this introductory paragraph of the official Presbyterian manual for the organization of Christian education in the local church:

> When the necessity for Christian education is properly understood and it is seen as the providing of the indispensable human channel through which God's grace and truth may reach

all men, at once it is evident that education of this kind is
the function of the church as a whole. . . . So *essential* and so
central is this educational responsibility to the very nature of
the gospel and of the church that no one can be truly a Christian and evade the burden of it.[1]

Yet when working as an educator within the church and
when observing the religious arena in periods of detachment,
this observer sensed a great divorce between the educational
rationale of the religious institution and the functional embodiment of these theological descriptions. This situation cried
for clarification.

A second puzzling phenomenon was that some literature
and many religious educators talked of the "rapidly expanding programs" and "the broadening scope" of educational interests under the sponsorship of the church. When Meland
wrote his account of adult education in the church back in
1939, one could easily get the impression that the boom in
adult education had already started and that before long the
church would adopt this "new frontier" on a broad scale.

Were a man of ancient or medieval times to saunter through
a modern city church or synagogue, as I have had occasion to
in recent months, he would be bewildered beyond understanding. Doors! Many of them, opening into rooms filled with
busy people—busy listening, hearing, or just "doing things."
On a tour one Tuesday evening through a prominent city church
on the West Coast, undoubtedly one of the most enterprising
parish centers along the Pacific, I counted not less than fifteen
doors that led into meetings of one kind or other.

"Here," said the minister, opening a door with obvious pride,
"are some of our people listening to a lecture on co-operatives."
. . . "In this room . . ."[2]

Others, however, were talking about "The Divine Constraint
of Christian Education for Adults."[3] Christian education was
not to go off in all directions on a broad scale! Yet, when
"divine constraint" was offered as an operating principle by

the clergymen it appeared to this observer that much under the label of "adult education" tended toward pure entertainment rather than education.

Furthermore, there appeared to be a good deal of tension within the religious institution as indicated in the high frequency of staff changes, widespread uneasiness and disappointment in the educator's role in the church, and the growing shortage of clergymen planning for this role or staying with it once in it. This had become strikingly apparent when the writer had announced his plan to do further graduate work in preparation for the role of minister of Christian education. One colleague bluntly stated: "Don't you know that you are going in the wrong direction? A man who can preach and administrate a parish ought not to be planning for the educational ministry." It appeared to this researcher that if this was a pervasive phenomenon, it would undoubtedly affect the quality and quantity of adult education.

To answer such problems as these, a growing body of research and theory has emerged in the sociology of religion[4] and the sociology of organizations and institutions.[5] Burton Clark had made a major contribution to adult education with an institutional analysis of adult education in the Los Angeles school system, and it appeared that a similar approach would not only apply emerging theory in these fields to another institutional situation but aid greatly in understanding Christian adult education as well as the religious institution.[6]

In this study the focus has been upon the behavior patterns of the participants in the religious enterprise, the pressures to which the church has been subjected, the values that have been altered by the necessities of organizational existence, special needs and problems that impinge upon the religious institution and affect its character, and the historical patterns of accommodation and adaptation.

Although the models in this report are not necessarily limited to the specific churches observed, nine churches in the San Francisco Bay Area were selected for special observation.

In the selection of churches no question concerning adult education was raised, for there was no interest in seeking outstanding examples of adult education or in drawing conclusions from special cases. Instead, the churches were selected with the following criteria:

1. Three organizational types of church polity were selected —congregational, presbyterian, and episcopal (as represented by the American Baptist Convention, The United Presbyterian Church in the U.S.A., and The Methodist Church).

2. Three urban settings were represented—downtown, suburban, and intermediate areas. The downtown churches were located in and around the central business district; suburban churches were located in the rapidly expanding fringes of the metropolitan area where new residential districts were being developed; and intermediate churches were selected from the older built-up residential districts.

3. The churches selected were modal churches of the particular denominations and the particular urban settings, in regard to membership, budget, and value of real estate.

4. Atypical institutions such as university churches with an unusually large contingent of students were not considered.

5. Established denominations were selected rather than sect groups because these denominations comprise the bulk of Protestantism and have a history of interest in adult education.

6. Denominations were selected that could provide "normal" churches in each of the urban settings.

7. The selections were made on the basis of accessibility, co-operation, and available resources.

In order to protect the identity of the churches involved we shall hereafter refer to the churches as designated below:

Downtown churches:

    1. First Baptist Church

    2. First Presbyterian Church

    3. First Methodist Church

Intermediate churches:

    4. Second Baptist Church

5. Second Presbyterian Church
6. Second Methodist Church

Suburban churches:

7. Third Baptist Church
8. Third Presbyterian Church
9. Third Methodist Church

Since institutional studies involve a search for significant factors in a complex situation of social behavior, a variety of methods were used. Questionnaires were utilized as much for exploratory purposes as for the substantiation of hypotheses. One questionnaire was used with ninety-eight adult group leaders, of which seventy-three (74.6 per cent) responded. An additional questionnaire yielded 1,001 respondents. Although precise information is not available, the loss here was very close to 15 per cent.

Open-ended interview schedules also yielded much information. Leads in these interviews were followed by pertinent, probing questions directed to bring out significant data.

Participant observation with the "participant as observer" was another basic method. This method is used when social scientists are especially interested in understanding a particular organization or substantive problem rather than demonstrating relations between abstractly defined variables. This is more commonly the case when researchers do not know enough about the organization a priori to identify relevant problems and hypotheses and when they must discover these in the course of the research. In this study the researcher was, most frequently, just another participant in the life of the church. He was known as an ordained clergyman only to the clergy, to a few other staff personnel, and late in the study, to a few select laymen. When an introduction was necessary he was described as a graduate student interested in adult education in the church. Beyond this, few explanations were required and these were guardedly vague.

Most of the participant observation was done in First Baptist Church, where the field worker found it easy to drop in for lunch with the staff, participate (along with his family) in the group life of the church, and also amble into congregational meetings as one of the group, although not formally a member. In such situations, "interviews" were picked up "on the hoof" and observations of persons in a variety of situations were made. When problems arose the researcher frequently was there to witness behavior.

Documentary analysis also provided significant insights into institutional problems and reliable information on organizational decisions. Minutes of meetings, church periodicals and letters, denominational and interdenominational annual reports, brochures, denominational curriculums and curriculum-servicing literature, and historical accounts were among the documents perused for available indices to problems and institutional characteristics.

One tough decision had to be made in the course of the research. Although there would undoubtedly have been some significant insights on differences of institutional clientele, urban setting, denominational affiliation, etc., the decision had to be made as to what would produce the most rewarding observations at this stage of the analysis about adult education in the church. Because the "big story" seemed to emerge out of the sociological common ground which these churches had in the organizational model of the religious institution in America, these enticing sidetracks were bypassed.

It is not intended that a sociological approach supplant, but rather *complement,* the traditional approaches. However, it has proved profitable for an adequate understanding of the disparity between the theological rationale for adult education and the limits of its embodiment, the illusion sometimes gained that adult education has a broad range with few institutional limitations, and the overly sold assumption that institutional character is determined by theological discipline without regard for numerous social determinants.

Adult educators in other fields will be interested in the fact that, once again, adult education is couched within, and dependent upon, a parent institution. As the religious institution has taken upon itself the organizational forms common to an industrial age, adult education can be functionally described as a specialized activity incidental to the main preoccupations of the religious enterprise. Objectives and values are implemented in contemporary organizational structures through specialized units with specialized functions. If we share a concern about these objectives and values, then we must, of necessity, consider the relationship of specialized functions to the total organism.

Students of social change will gain an appreciation of the forces that impinge upon the religious institution. To say that social change in one institutional sphere has repercussions on other areas is now axiomatic. This is especially significant since the church is a conservative, "old-line" institution with numerous built-in rigidities to resist change. Seldom has there been an age demanding more adaptation and accommodation. If we do not focus upon the behavior characteristics of the religious institution in the midst of change, we miss the determinants and may be unappreciative of the real stress and strain. This has been well stated by Burton Clark:

> Organizations do not adjust automatically to a changing environment. Variations in adjustment patterns and in sharpness of response may be anticipated on the grounds of differences in organizational needs and interests. Or, similarities may be expected where basic factors are common to a number of organizations. The problem of institutional change in modern society is frequently a problem in organizational dynamics. Unless we utilize an institutional perspective, we miss important immediate causes of institutional change, or, of more consequence, we miss the intervening variables that may well be the most important determinants of change.[7]

The sociological approach also provides churchmen with further clarification of problems of institutional leadership. Many times churchmen are not aware of the general drift into an entirely different type of religious institution even when they are a part of it. Although some churchmen are aware of some of the corrupting consequences of secular society, like any institutional leadership, they have difficulty in identifying and controlling the changes that take place within the church. When the problems of institutional leadership are not understood, the *integrity of the institution is endangered* through an unconscious drift into uncompromising discrepancies between theological definitions of purpose and their functional embodiment. It is the writer's conviction that this is precisely the case in the church.

The general finding of this research is that the program of adult education in the church reflects the character of the religious institution as a whole. Adult education takes its character from the forces that impinge upon the religious institution in American society and it functions to serve the religious institution according to the needs and the problems of the hour. Although in recent years more has been said about the philosophy and theology of education (and more specifically adult education) the emerging rationale does not affect the character of adult education as significantly as the operating pressures that intervene between the aspirations of mission and role and the actual classroom. In brief, the embodiment of mission fails to materialize as desired largely because of unexamined sociological characteristics both internal and external.

In the identification of these characteristics we notice that the pattern of institutional servicing has been the general pattern through the history of the church (Chapter I), that the marginality of the church in American society gives distinctive coloring to the adult education it offers, and the internal marginality of the educational phases of church life proves to be a weak base from which to develop (Chapter II). Ample indices of social differentiation were found which provide the religious institution with distinctive clientele from one setting to another (Chapter III). Interdenominational bodies, dependent upon co-operative resources, have been limited in the adult education they sponsor, although some fine adult education has been realized. The bureaucratization of denominational bodies has made adult education a specialty function that gains access to the public primarily through adopting and aiding the general goals and current needs of the religious organization (Chapter IV). Local associations on the front lines of a geographically dispersed enterprise find that the need for institutional security is such a major problem that adult education under its sponsorship is markedly colored by this need (Chapter V). Here more than any other place adult education must service institutional need. In some cases it must give way to other functions which do a better job of building security.

A further word of warning needs to be stated before the reader plunges into the body of the report. Numerous findings will be considered negative by the reader. The researcher has not considered this a "cloak-and-dagger" debunking of the religious institution, and it is hoped that others will not see it as such. Nevertheless, there are times when it is profitable to "look at the devil with fascinated eye" if we are to know where the battle line is drawn. This is a report by a concerned churchman. No derogatory terminology has been intended. Although the writer may have succumbed to some facetiousness here and there, a term such as "bureaucracy" has no pejorative intent or invidious connotations, but is technically derived.

Chapter I

THE BACKGROUND OF ADULT EDUCATION IN THE CHURCH

O NE OF THE characteristics that has made adult education under the sponsorship of the church different from adult education under the sponsorship of many other kinds of agencies is the fact that the church has had a long, evolving history. Adult education has played a significant role in its development through the centuries. In such an old-line institution there have been many traditions established and rigidities implanted in the very fiber of the institution to the extent that changes do not come easily. Nevertheless, adaptation and accommodation have taken place again and again, often at a much slower pace than that demanded by some of the participants. Therefore, schism has split the church into many separate institutions that carry on a ministry to different types of people who look for satisfactions in different kinds of religious experiences.

Besides the characteristics that reflect the long history of the church, there are others that reflect the peculiar needs and problems that the church must satisfy to keep it viable. In other words, the educational program of the church is one aspect of church life that may be focused to maintain institutional security.

It is to emphasize and give substance to these characteristics that this chapter is written. Since it is not the purpose of the author to write a detailed history of organizational accommodation, a highly selective approach has been made.

EDUCATION AND INSTITUTIONAL DEVELOPMENT

The character of adult education has reflected the developmental stages of the religious institution and the particular problems of each social situation. A few high lights of this ongoing process are recalled here to accent the marked variations that have occurred.

Education and the founding of a movement. As is common to the founders of the world's great religions, the Founder of Christianity was one who came teaching ethical spiritual ideals that would be most perfectly embodied in a "Kingdom" created by the power of God rather than by the skill of man. Jesus, a practicing Jew and carpenter by trade, took over a role of itinerant teacher. Reports Lewis Sherrill:

> Now if one's patience can endure some counting of words, the results may repay the tedium. The word "Teacher" is used forty-two times in the Gospels with reference to Jesus, thirty-five instances being in the Synoptics and seven in John. In thirty-one of these forty-two instances, he is directly addressed as "Teacher"; six of these are in Matthew, ten in Mark, twelve in Luke, and three in John. He is reported as referring to himself as Teacher, in five instances. Other forms of address equivalent to Teacher also appear fourteen times—Rabbi twelve times, and Rabboni twice. Thus he is called Teacher, or the equivalent of that term, sixty-one times in the Gospels.[1]

It is also of note that the teaching of Jesus was not due to the impulse of a social movement. Ernst Troeltsch, in his monumental study, *The Social Teachings of the Christian Churches,* states this directly when he writes:

> To put it quite plainly: Christianity was not the product of a class struggle of any kind; it was not shaped, when it did arise,

in order to fit into any such situation: indeed, at no point was it directly concerned with the social upheavals of the ancient world. The fact, however, remains that Jesus addressed himself primarily to the oppressed, and to the "little ones" of the human family, that he considered wealth a danger to the soul, and that he opposed the Jewish priestly aristocracy which represented the dominant ecclesiastical forces of his day. It is also clear that the early church sought and won her new adherents chiefly among the lower classes in the cities, and that members of the well-to-do, educated upper classes only began to enter the church in the second century, and then only gradually: and we are aware that this change did not take place without a good deal of opposition on the part of the educated and wealthy sections of society.[2]

Thus it was that the central theme was a purely religious one with Jesus. Although the literature of the Christian church has dealt exhaustively with his message, it is more profitable for our purposes to acknowledge the lack of any class struggle in its origin and let the matter rest.

As far as organizational structure to the movement goes, there seems to be little evidence of an extensive and systematic organization. His public career was brief (no more than three years and quite possibly compressed within a year), and as far as surviving records show, he gave little thought to a continuing organization to perpetrate his teachings. He gathered around him a group of intimate disciples, and some have reported that he entrusted them with great powers which he intended to be transmitted to succeeding generations; but this has been hotly debated, and there is no certain proof of the issue in any of the early documents.

In general, we get the picture of the Founder as an itinerant teacher who gathered about him a select group of intimate disciples, developing in these teachings no single social problem of the age but rather an ethical and spiritual orientation to the broad scope of life which would eventually culminate in the coming of the "Kingdom of God." In the main, the teachings appealed to the lower classes, who had felt the pressures of contemporary society most acutely. There was little in the way of pressure to found and perpetuate an ongoing institution. As a consequence the teachings were never issued systematically, but as the occasion required—at dinner parties, to the lepers along the road, to the woman at the well.

Education and institutionalization.[3] At the time of the martyrdom of the Founder, the loosely knit body of Christian believers, waiting in Jerusalem "for the promise of the Father" and preparing for the Kingdom of God, was anything but a stable religious organization. It wasn't long, however, before this rather obscure sect of Judaism developed an expansive institution that spread across the Greco-Roman world. As this came about, a number of interesting phenomena emerged.

First, the casual, unsystematized teachings of Jesus became an idealized framework from which the followers of Jesus began to effect an organization in concrete social settings. With the concept of equality of men before God implicit in Jesus' teachings, new communities were organized where radical social and religious experimentation was in existence. With little but the memory of the Martyr and what was described as coming "in power and in the Holy Spirit," austere radicalism and unlimited individualism gained a freedom of expression without precedent. In time, stability was to be found and "proper" Christian living was to be defined more clearly, but this is the stuff of which the adult education of the hour was made. How were they to deal with private property in a life that was shortly to be transformed through divine intervention? How should Christians live in a community of love? What should be the state of marriage and family? What did brotherhood mean when some form of social stratification seemed necessary to the ongoing society? What was to be the relationship of the Christian community to the synagogue? How should their daily affairs be organized? The New Testament comes alive with these issues and we can well imagine the heat with which they were debated.

Early there appeared a vigorous, proselytizing message (*kērygma*) directed principally to the Jews but later to the Gentiles. But a ministry of teaching followed quickly upon the heels of the vigorous recruitment to establish the neophytes in the faith. Lewis Sherrill has identified five different kinds of teaching[4] and several types of writing[5] from which the teaching of the early church was done.

In the midst of all this zealous early growth there was an interesting development and reshuffling of leadership, and we can feel quite certain that as the leadership changed in the early church the message took on a distinctive reflection of that role. Among those who embody some special gift (*charisma*) the apostle was the first person to strike out in the establishment of Christian churches. For the most part, the apostles were dependent upon the various churches to which they ministered. As congregations became established, local prophets emerged to whom the local church now gave increasing attention and support. The major difference between these two leadership positions was that the apostle had no permanent place of domicile but the prophet became the spokesman for the local community. A third leader arose in the Christian community and was simply called "teacher" (*didaskalos*). He was also expected to have a charismatic gift of spiritual knowledge and was given a special place in the public meeting where he conducted his teaching.

To these three leadership positions there were later added bishops, presbyters, and deacons by election in the local church as needs arose and further division of responsibilities became necessary.

The first of these offices to fade away was that of the apostle. Undoubtedly the fact that he had little or no control over the local church, which could easily wean away his support and look with favor upon one of its own local sons, the prophet, has much to do with it. However, itinerant men with charismatic gifts were appearing long after the middle of the second century. In the end both prophets and teachers were faced with the same oblivion, but they were reportedly in some form of conflict with the elected clergy until the fourth century. Undoubtedly the fact that the bishop took over the chief administrative functions, including the care of income and expenses, was an important factor in his emergence as the most significant of the previously mentioned offices. The zealous proselytizing by the spiritually gifted began to defer to the elected officials whose energies were more frequently spent upon the building of somewhat more conservative, ordered communities that could exist in an increasingly hostile world.

Institutional roles continued to develop and take on varying characteristics through the centuries. As "the development of orderly, stable, socially integrating forms and structures" emerged through the process of institutionalization, striking changes in the character of the church and marked alterations in roles took place at a much slower pace. In fact, as the church settled down for the long pull to eternity it took tremendous pressures, staggering problems, and extreme cultural differences over extensive periods of time to change the nature of the religious institution. Once the formation of the institutional character took place, dramatic and cataclysmic crises were necessary to override the resultant conservatism, formalized roles, vested interests, infused values, and the distinctive characteristics of a particular social composition and social base.

There is a long leap between the organizational forces that became solidified in the more fluid early period of organizational development in the church, and the beginning of the "Ragged School" by Robert Raikes in 1780, in England. Yet we do not understand the institutional problems of contemporary educational functions in the church unless we see something such as this in relation to the process of institutionalization that preceded it.

The introduction of the educational endeavors of the Sunday school movement have evidently not been cataclysmic enough to change many of the institutionalized patterns of the Christian church. From the very beginning, the Sunday school movement was seen as a threat to the church. It was seen as a sign of stirring among the common people that might even have revolutionary implications. (What would happen when the proletariat became educated and were no longer willing to maintain their humble place in society?) The whole enterprise was seen as an anticlerical movement and was forced to operate completely outside the scope and authority of the church in the beginning. In a word, the church could not alter its institutional structure to incorporate this new ministry and developed a rationale for its traditional patterns. What was true in England had its counterpart in America.

Even today the Sunday school is still something of an innovation within the church. This newness contributes significantly to the marginality of the educational enterprise of the religious institution. As we shall see later, the values associated with the educational processes are precarious and the leadership necessary to administrate the program is in a weak position within the structure. Thus, historically, the contemporary educational enterprise of the religious institution, most commonly associated with the Sunday school, is not institutionally secure. The religious institution follows the historical pattern of all old-line social institutions in that changes come much more easily during the early periods of emerging development than in the later periods of conservative self-maintenance.

Institutionalization plays a very significant role in the understanding of the niche that adult education takes within the religious enterprise. We have already seen that the more relaxed, casual teaching of the Founder changed when the application of these ideals began to take form and meet problems in concrete situations during the early period of institutional development. As the radical experimentation, inspired by charismatic personalities, gave way to a more conservative, ordered institution, under the leadership of those whose charisma was derived from their office,[6] education became even more concerned with stable organizational existence and less radical expression. However, after the institution had established itself and solidified its values and behavior patterns, innovations were only slowly accommodated. Such has been the fate of the more recent endeavors in religious education.

Education and institutional marginality. An interesting story of the redirection of education to meet organizational needs relates to the changing status of the church as it moved from the tombs to the throne. Indeed it was not until the espousal of Christianity by Constantine in the fourth century that the severe persecution of the Christians was relaxed. Off and on during these early centuries, confessing Christians did not know if they were going to celebrate the shedding of Christ's blood in the Eucharist or if they were going to spill their own blood as a price for their membership in this new sect. "Indeed, with the possible exception of Judaism, Christianity has had more martyrs than any other religion."[7]

Not only was the church challenged directly by persecution from the state that drove it for a time into the catacombs, but it was also challenged by a complex inner world of religions and philosophies. The Christian gospel had to be interpreted against the background of the Greco-Roman world, in which there was usually one "state" religion and many other religious cults generally called "mystery religions." Although it is almost impossible to say with finality what Christianity gave to the mystery religions and what it took over from them, it can hardly be doubted that there was assimilation from this source.

As one might expect, the adult education of the period was deeply colored by the banks through which the troubled stream of institutional development ran. The teaching function in the church passed into the hands of elected ministers along with other functions. But perhaps the most distinctive development was that of catechetical instruction, in the face of challenges by competing ideologies and state persecution.

The catechumenate, which was devised for adult converts, directed its instruction toward the disciplining of the moral life, the acquainting of the catechumen with the Christian tradition, and the creation of a profound devotion to the Christian faith and way of life.[8] It functioned to introduce the adults into the Christian "army."[9] This militant ideal was very strong until about the fourth century. Christians considered themselves soldiers of Christ and their baptism as "enlistment" with him. The baptism was a *sacramentum,* or pledge, the spiritual equivalent of a military oath. The catechumenate was a proving ground for the larger action against the foes of Christian forces.

The catechumenate may be traced in its growth and then in its decline. In the second century it was still indistinct in many of its details, but in the years from about 200 to 325 considerable development occurred. Three distinct states have been reported in evidence during this period: (1) a stage involving a preliminary inquiry and private instruction, (2) a stage in which the neophyte is admitted to the first part of the Christian worship service and instructed privately as a class, (3) a stage in which there is further inquiry and more intensive instruction just prior to baptism.[10]

In the period from about 325 to 450 the catechumenate reached the peak of its development. However, with the coming of the church to a position of power as the official state religion of the Roman Empire, the widespread acceptance of the Christian church, and the throngs of people who affiliated with the church in the post-Constantinian era, it is significant that the catechumenate began to decline in importance. With the lessening of threats from the state and the mystery religions, the need for a militant recruitment and indoctrination of "soldiers for Christ" also began to diminish. Then, with the disintegration of the state, the church enjoyed even more complete autonomy as a politico-religious society with growing control over its members.

As the need for a strong militant organization gave way and all kinds of people thronged to the baptismal fount, instruction gave way to an emphasis on the sacrament of Baptism, and the church turned to its new task of justifying in theology the symbolic educational meaning which the baptismal ceremony now had. Frequently a series of liturgical acts were carried out, through which the candidate was "instructed" in the Gospels, the creed, and the Lord's Prayer. Liturgical acts originally designed for adults were eventually transferred to infants. Some, such as the symbolic examination of the ear openings of the child for prebaptismal examination, were also fabricated as magical rituals to serve this purpose. The period of catechetical instruction began to shrink as ritual came in to take its place. By the seventh century the period of instruction had virtually disappeared in the west.

In these brief historical descriptions we have seen that *as the institutional needs and problems of the Christian church changed form, the type of adult education also differed to meet these varying situations.* We have seen that under the casual, relaxed, unsystematized teachings of the Founder, who seemed to have no organizational pressures to cope with except those of the informal group of friends, adult education was vastly different from what it was in other periods. Under the severe persecution of the Roman Caesars when the militant organization demanded an elaborate and involved catechetical program to protect itself from external annihilation and internal betrayal, adult education functioned to meet the threats of the age. Adult education was also vastly different in the church when the apostle's charismatic personality and message were needed to inspire proselytes with a vision of a better life, and when the elected officials in local communities had the responsibility for ordering and stabilizing the "community of love" which had known the excesses of freedom, license, and radical experimentation. *Yet at all times it was religious education in the sense that it was directed to the needs of the religious institution.* Each of these changes in adult education, which reflect so definitely the needs and problems of the church as an institution, provide us with a valuable clue for the analysis of contemporary adult education in the church.

On the other hand, when the church is required to alter its internal structure in order to incorporate a new ministry, the likelihood of any quick change, after the institutional form has solidified, is nil. Such changes require long periods of time and threats to the institutional security if the accommodation is to be made.

Such was the fate of the Sunday school movement of the eighteenth century. We can expect this fate to be shared by any innovation in educational program which is not readily seen to meet the institutional needs and problems of the religious institution.

ORGANIZATIONAL DIFFERENTIATION

Schism.[11] The Christian community never sailed far from the shore before it was in the deep water of dissent, as even the sketchiest reading of the New Testament will reveal. Dissent called for the vigorous attention and theological formulations like that of Paul in his letter to the Ephesians. The ecumenical councils of Nicaea, Constantinople, Ephesus, and Chalcedon bear witness to the difficulties inherent in the divisions of the great sees of Antioch, Alexandria, Rome, Jerusalem, and Constantinople. The controversies over the person of Christ, the "watery unions" of the seventh century, the excommunication of the Patriarch Michael Cerularius, and the hatred displayed in the sack of Constantinople by the Crusades, all bear witness to the significance of "the great schism." Although more research will be necessary to tell the full story, it has long been clear that heresy had the upper hand for generations in some of the richest provinces of the south of France and even in Italy itself, and that the Catholic Church was almost at the point of disappearance in these locations during the supposedly harmonious medieval period.[12] The account of religious dissent in the Western church during the Protestant Reformation is more commonly known.

Although schism found widespread acceptance in sixteenth-century Europe, nothing comparable to what we have in the United States can be met anywhere in the world. The *Yearbook of American Churches* of 1959[13] lists 251 religious bodies with a membership of 109,557,741, and many other small religious groups are not included in these figures. The ecclesiastical map of the United States has been likened to "the old patchwork crazy quilts that American grandmothers used to prize so highly—a coverlet of disparate patches, put together without regard for an over-all pattern, but aesthetic according to Grandmother's ways of thinking."[14] H. Richard Niebuhr has undoubtedly given us the best discussion of this process when he focused upon the four factors—race, class, sectionalism, and nationalism.[15]

Adaptation and accommodation. As we turn to the other side of the coin we must know something about the polar types of "church" and "sect" first identified by Max Weber but more amply defined by Ernst Troeltsch.[16] Troeltsch defined the church as being a "natural" institution into which the individual is born and trained in the religious community. The church accepts the secular social order and becomes dependent upon its patterns of stratification and general conservatism. Duly constituted ecclesiastical officials make up its priestly hierarchy, which perpetuates its traditions, administers its sacraments, and vests its authority in a charisma of office. The sect, on the other hand, is a voluntary association which is likely to demand of its membership some definite type of religious experience as a prerequisite. Rather than identifying with and dominating the secular world the sect may become indifferent, intolerant, or even antagonistic toward the secular world. Instead, an independent moral community sufficient unto itself emerges and calls forth an untrained leadership that draws authority from a direct appeal to Scripture, special revelation, moral discipline, and the charisma of personality. The sect usually draws its members from the lower classes in contrast to the church, which is constituted mainly from the middle and upper classes.

Perhaps one of the most interesting phenomena of the sect-church typology is the fact that the sect *moves* in the course of its history to a more church-type position. This tends to close rather than widen the gap between religious expressions. Reports H. Richard Niebuhr:

> By its very nature the sectarian type of organization is valid only for one generation. The children born to the voluntary members of the first generation begin to make the sect a church long before they have arrived at the years of discretion. For with their coming the sect must take on the character of an educational and disciplinary institution, with the purpose of bringing the new generation into conformity with the ideals and customs which have become traditional.[17]

Analyzed by Liston Pope in his study of Gaston County, North Carolina, twenty-one indices of movement were identified to indicate the various facets of this tradition.[18]

Besides the accommodation that takes place in the movement from sect to church there are also significant signs of emerging unity in American society. Robert Lee,[19] in an attempt to reapply the insights of H. Richard Niebuhr's four-factor analysis, asserts the reduction of social differences of race, class, sectionalism, and nationalism so pronounced heretofore. He further identifies mass communication, common values, styles of life, mutual dependence, organizational revolution, and symbols of national unity as forces diminishing social divisiveness. Although this writer believes that Lee has underestimated the genius of the human being to find new sources of differentiation when old ones become blurred, his basic observation concerning these traditional indices is generally sound.

A number of keen observers have declared an increasing secularism as the price paid for accommodation to the environment. Martin E. Marty talks of "the erosion of particularity, the smoothing of the edges of witness, the loss of religious content."[20] Will Herberg states that it is "the American Way of Life that supplies American society with an 'overarching sense of unity' amid conflict."[21] J. Milton Yinger states, "The 'return to religion' can be understood only by noting the simultaneous secularization of the church."[22] Robin Williams has pointed out that Americans are not irreligious, but that there has been a withdrawal of "affect," of pervasive emotional involvement with traditional religions.[23] Such secularism does not support schismatic tendencies, although its lack of involvement does not actively break down institutional barriers.

Sociopsychological sources of religious differentiation. Although certain recent developments appear to work toward a sociological common ground as the basis of church unity (further observations of socioreligious differentiation will be made in Chapter III) the persistent pressures of dissent and division have been with the church from the beginning. Unfortunately, when historians have identified these new religious movements they have described primarily the political influences that have been related to the theological controversies. As a consequence we have grown to think of some theological or liturgical dispute as the major cause of these divisions. Elmer Clark, writing in *The Ecumenical Review,* put the matter correctly when he wrote:

> It thus appears that the great and well-known theological issues, which are so earnestly debated at top levels by those who are striving for unity among the church, are not the only or even the main factors which have operated to create and maintain disunity. The real causes are to be sought elsewhere. This is,

of course, not to say that the theological issues are unimportant and do not merit the emphasis placed upon them. It does mean, however, that even if such issues were all settled Christian unity would not be achieved, nor would we be able to discern political influences even in the great theological disputes between East and West, between Rome and the Reformer, and in the process by which Anglicanism diverged from Rome. Sociological and psychological forces of varied nature complicate the present pattern of a disrupted church, and these forces may be more difficult to discern and adjust than the diverse theologies which vex us. Without ceasing to explore the matters of faith and order, the ecumenical leadership should begin to delve into the problem of economies, temperament, church pride, personality, and deep human hungers, and the whole complex pattern of the mental make-up and social relationship of man.[24]

Earlier in this century a number of now classic studies began to open up the psychological and sociological areas of religious expression. The Gifford Lectures of William James have now become widely known as *The Varieties of Religious Experience*.[25] Although this famous philosopher tended to delve into the "extremes" of religious expression, he awakened an interest in the psychological as an explanation for religious differences. A little later Ernst Troeltsch published his *The Social Teachings of the Christian Churches*,[26] which documented a tremendous range in the development of Christian social ethics. In short order, Emile Durkheim launched his quest for the source of religion and announced in his *The Elementary Forms of Religious Life*[27] that it was to be found in society itself. Not so controversial has been H. Richard Niebuhr's *The Social Sources of Denominationalism*.[28] These studies, as well as others, have served to direct attention to the growing realization that sociological and psychological factors are to be considered as "real causes" of religious differentiation. Slowly, but with increasing pace, the skeleton is being filled in by the social scientists, and some important sources of differentiation are breaking into the language and literature of the churchmen.[29]

One of the interesting examples of this movement to real causes is the direct dealing with the issue by both Greenslade and Yinger. Greenslade, acknowledging the "social sources of H. Richard Niebuhr and emphasizing the personal conflicts among leaders," studied the splits that occurred frequently in the ranks of Christendom in the first few centuries and listed five causes of schism in the early church: (1) personal, (2) national, social, and economic, (3) rivalry of sees, (4) liturgical disputes, and (5) problems of discipline and the Puritan idea of the church.[30]

But Yinger rightly discerns that it is necessary to ask *"why* some take this side of a liturgical dispute, and some another, *who* defends most vigorously the need for church discipline and who the opposing doctrine of prophetic inspiration."[31] With such a functional analysis as a basis, Yinger moves on to a somewhat larger system which is highly interactive and mutually reinforcing:

1. Variation in personal religious needs and interests, due to differences in basic personality tendencies, in the strength of feeling of frustration and guilt, in level of intellectual development, in capacity for certain kinds of religious experience, etc.

2. Variations in economic and political interests.

3. National differences.

4. Social mobility and social change.

5. Differences that derive from the internal development of the religious system.[32]

This, of course, is no terminal point either, but the "why" and the "who" questions of the social scientists mark a significant turn in the road and are filled with potential insight.

Backgrounds of adult education in the church. The orientation of this study is likewise dependent upon a functional analysis of religious behavior with special emphasis upon the institutional character of the religious organization, and in this chapter we have begun that analysis. If others in the rapidly expanding adult education movement are to understand what niche the church has carved out for itself in this movement and how it is likely to develop in the future, it is necessary to appraise the characteristics of the organizational setting in which the church expresses itself. If churchmen are to understand this long-standing phase of church work, they must see its dependence upon organizational needs and problems. If they desire to give it new direction, they must of necessity go beyond naïve aspirations and resolutions and *effect changes in the institutional structure,* which in many cases will mean radical surgery and postoperative repercussions.

In this chapter the groundwork for such an undertaking has begun. First, *the church has been described as an old-line institution with adult education playing a significant role in the institution from the very beginning.* It is an organization that has been deeply infused with value and rationale. In such an institution, built-in rigidities mediate against sudden changes. Therefore one would not expect adult education to change from day to day as it might under the young, nascent, emerging organizational structure of the public schools.[33] Adaptation and accommodation does take place, as in the movement from sectlike to churchlike institutions, but this is at a much slower pace than that of the clientele.

Since sociological and psychological changes take place in society at a faster pace than organizational changes, there have been many schisms to divide the religious establishment into many different organizational structures and substructures. Although theological differences play an important part in defining differences, the social and psychological sources of denominationalism have been accented here as "real" causes frequently overlooked.

Furthermore, *as institutional need and problems of church changed, the types of adult education also changed to meet these varying needs.* This characteristic suggests that adult education under the sponsorship of the church gains its directives from sources other than the purely educational and that education is in a subservient or marginal relationship to other interests. In the following chapter we will attempt to define this position and identify the dependency patterns.

Chapter II

MARGINALITY AND THE
RELIGIOUS INSTITUTION

FOR AN APPRAISAL of adult education in the church it is necessary to understand something of the marginal position of the church in American society and the marginality of education within the religious institution itself. Any appraisal of what the church has been doing in the past, what it is doing today, and what adult education is likely to become in the future is colored by this marginality, for it doesn't seem likely that this limitation will be overcome in the foreseeable future.

MARGINALITY OF THE CHURCH IN AMERICAN SOCIETY

Perhaps it seems strange to the reader that an accent is placed upon the marginality of religion in America when the current decade has witnessed an all-time high in the upswing of religious interest.[1] This contemporary picture of a "return to religion" gains support from survey data,[2] church membership statistics,[3] and church construction figures[4] as well as the popularity of religious personages, literature, movies, and jukebox favorites. States Will Herberg: "That there has in recent years been an upswing in religion in the United States can hardly be doubted; the evidence is diverse, converging, and unequivocal beyond all possibilities of error."[5]

Yet throughout this whole phenomenon of revival, the religious as well as the secular leaders in America have been skeptical about the impact of religion upon the critical decisions of American life.[6] This was also the response of the ministers in this study. One clergyman in a downtown church declared:

> This whole business of the religious revival is full of contradiction. More and more the church is shunted off to the periphery. More and more the important decisions are not being made by church people, nor are they being asked for a voice. I can't think of any major decision in this city where the church has had a voice.[7]

Though it seems at first glance to be an institution of power and influence, the church in America must admittedly recognize its marginal position. Although it is difficult to assess organizational marginality precisely, several contemporary symptoms of the church's peripheral status can be cited in such an appraisal.

Lack of establishment. Some evidence of marginality is indicated by the fact that there is *no established church in America.* Obviously the change in character of American religion conditioned by the lack of establishment represents both "gains" and "losses" to the religious enterprise.[8] The main point here is that toleration of numerous religious systems and secular frames of reference became an absolute necessity amid the pluralism of the New World. Although religious institutions might multiply with new freedom and competitive incentives, and perhaps even increase total institutional affiliation, the *shift in dependency* from the state to the public in a pluralistic society encouraged the secularization of the sacred and the fragmentation of the religious enterprise, of which we will have more to say. Dependency upon an increasingly secularized and pluralistic culture acted to increase the marginality of the religious enterprise in America. No longer could it speak to the people from a position of independence and power; and when it spoke to the state, its unanimity was shattered by its own pluralism, and its prophetic character was threatened by its dependency upon its increasingly secular social base.

The first clause of the Bill of Rights, prohibiting the establishment of a state church, was born out of social conditions that characterized the colonial period of American history. The colonial churches were largely transplanted by religious radicals[9] who differed with their old world antecedents but nevertheless zealously worked to establish their brand of religion in the new world. The variegated religious composition of the dissenting Protestant sects, the sizable Catholic minority, and a few Jewish people made the political consensus of *one* church impossible. Out of this heterogeneity, therefore, emerged the separation of church and state.[10]

This unique departure introduced a new principle into the intercourse of religion and the state[11] and is centrally important for the total character of religion in this country.[12] Williams, reflecting on the consequences, states:

> It was both the product and the cause of denominationalism, with its attendant evangelism, and imposed on the churches the necessity of competitive financing through voluntary contributions. It also encouraged lay representation and control in church organizations, as opposed to control by an ecclesiastical hierarchy, and facilitated local independence and secession tendencies in the individual denominations. It tended to reduce the symbolic reinforcement of mutually supportive political and religious organization. This eventually encouraged jealous defensiveness among Protestant sects against the state. Although the Catholic churches (and to a lesser degree, the Lutheran denominations) have not held this attitude strongly, they also have been profoundly affected by lack of establishment.[13]

Thus it was that while religious "liberty" was being secured in America, it altered its dependency on the state to dependency on the public, which tended to fragment its unity and reflect its manifold and increasingly secular publics. This more than any other historical development has influenced the institutional character of religion in America.

Denominational fragmentation. As cited earlier, the *Yearbook of American Churches* lists 251 religious bodies in the United States and gives support to what Sperry has called the "religious fecundity" of our society. However, there are 82 religious bodies each having over 50,000 members and reporting 98.4 per cent of the total number of members. Many of these denominations, in what has been called America's "ecclesiastical zoo," have been importations from other countries, especially Europe, for the immigrants who peopled the original thirteen colonies brought with them their distinctive types of church life and organization.[14] Yet many defections and subdivisions of the earlier denominations have been indigenous to this country, emphasizing again the fact that America seems to provide an ideal spawning ground for the proliferation of sectarian religious bodies, beyond anything known elsewhere in Christendom.

From the standpoint of organizational efficiency the denominational system is an extremely inefficient form of organizational engineering.[15] If the church had developed under a centralized authority, rather than breaking asunder with schisms throughout its history, the delegation of responsibility for the various phases of institutional expression would have been radically different from the organization that the church now has in its various denominations. Long before the phasic partition had been exhausted, the organizational structure of the church developed multiple organizations without providing an authoritative administration or the necessary auxiliary services to all constituent enterprises.[16]

There can be little doubt that this denominational pluralism has added to the marginality of the religion in America. One eminent Protestant leader has declared, "It appears indisputable that Protestantism, during the past two or three generations, has been actually and startlingly declining from its long ascendant position in American life."[17] Not only must we agree, but we must assert that his time span is too short. The fragmentation of the religious enterprise in America has weakened its program, undermined its authority, and dissipated its energies into the day-by-day demands of institutional survival. Continues Morrison:

> A disunited church is no match for the tremendous power of the social collectives that have emerged in modern America. This is the lesson that we should learn from our half century's abortive attempt to implement the social gospel. Our American society has completely changed its form as compared with the simplicities of the age of individualism. Great magnitudes of social organization have emerged, over against which our denominational churches present a picture of limp futility. Protestantism has not learned to live in the modern world. It has carried over from the era of individualism its atomistic and autonomous sectarian organizations and the simple procedures which seemed appropriate in that era, but are so no longer. Everything has changed—the whole structure of society—but Protestantism is compelled by its denominationalism to proceed as if it were living in the middle eighties of the nineteenth century.[18]

There can be little doubt that there is a wasteful expenditure of resources, when in every town, village, or city one can find numerous examples of small churches, frequently just across the street from each other, putting forth almost identical programs of church life and struggling with the severe limitations associated with insufficient size. But even beyond the wastefulness of overlapping local churches, denominational organizations also duplicate their overhead, in denominational headquarters that render similar services to local churches. In the area of education alone one is appreciably impressed with the multiplicity of expenditures in producing and printing separate but similar denominational literature. For an institution that affirms an ethical stewardship of all God-given resources, there is most certainly an incongruity in the denominational system.

But if such marked incongruities exist in the denominational system in spite of acknowledged marginality, there certainly must be some powerful organizational rigidities in the system that perpetuates it. Not the least of these is the "transformation of the relatives of history into eternal patterns and principles."[19] What is meaningful to a particular group of people in an organization at one time becomes overinvested with importance and perpetuates a whole "reign of error," as the specious validity of social beliefs fathers social realities in another age. Undoubtedly many such rigidities in the traditions of religious institutions are subject to the theorem of W. I. Thomas, which states: "If men define situations as real, they are real in their consequences." This theorem had been appropriately called the "self-fulfilling prophecy"[20] and may work for both organizational security and insecurity at the same time. In the case of religious denominationalism, it builds and perpetuates denominational security through the indoctrination of traditions and theological rationale that become even more firmly fixed in ritual and ceremony. At the same time it works toward the marginality of all denominations that go down together.

Closely related to the self-fulfilling prophecy is the whole matter of organizational fictions[21] that are *real and necessary to* all institutions (religious institutions are no exception). Certainly the ecumenical movement could profit from a functional analysis of organizational fictions in the denominational system, though frequently they are a bitter pill for the indoctrinated to accept.

Another group of insights that explain the rigidities of the denominational system come from the study of bureaucracy.[22] As Walter Muelder has helpfully pointed out:

> Church bureaucrats dominate ecumenical discussions. On the one hand, they wish the ecumenical movement to penetrate from the clerical bureaucracy to the laity. On the other hand, they are afraid that it will; for, as a consequence, one bureaucratic "elite" may be replaced by another.[23]

As the literature in the area of bureaucracy points out, vocational security tends to be secured and technical efficiency promoted. Administrative officers are secured through ritual and ceremony and regularized procedures are defined for movement up the ladder of increasingly valuable pensions, tenure, salaries, etc. At the same time administrational efficiency is actually increased through the perfection of control, continuity, rational order, and a carefully defined (often through informal procedures) system of authority. In the process of bureaucratization the layman (particularly the unindoctrinated) finds that he is farther and farther from the source of administrative decisions. When he does have influence in the pyramid of power it is that of protest rather than that of full initiative. Thus, the rigidities of the denominational system become more and more secure as those persons with high value infusion become responsible for decisions of denominational security.

Without delving farther into the mechanisms of denominationalism we can understand that the fragmenting consequences of religious pluralism are not only contributing to the marginality of religion in American society, but they are also firmly rooted. Such an understanding can help us become sympathetic with the interdenominational officer who lamented, "Things are apt to get much worse before they get much better."

Loss of ministerial authority. Another indication of marginality of religion in American society concerns the loss of ministerial authority in the secular arena. However, there seems to be some confusion at this point in the literature. Although generally acknowledging the fact that "religion in America seems to possess little capacity for rising above the relatives and ambiguities of the national consciousness,"[24] Will Herberg also states, "The enhanced standing of the churches and religion among the American people is strikingly indicated by the enhanced status of religious leaders."[25] Herberg supports his thesis with survey data from the opinion polls of Elmo Roper in 1942, 1947, and 1953. In answer to the question, "Which one of these groups do you feel is doing the most good for the country at the present time?" religious leaders jumped from third place in 1942 to first place in 1947 and 1953 with percentages 17.5, 32.6, and 40 respectively.[26]

> The picture of the clergyman that Americans have may not be without its ambiguous aspects, but there can be little doubt that the "minister of God" ranks high, and is rising rapidly, in the American scale of prestige. This rise of public confidence in clergymen no doubt reflects the rising status of religion and the church in American society.[27]

On the other hand, Stanley H. Chapman has described the minister as being in a declining status position. Tracing the evolution of the ministerial role from colonial days when "the ministry was both functionally and by status a part of the community leadership," through the eighteenth and nineteenth centuries to contemporary society, Chapman compares the ministerial role to that of the philosopher from which specific areas of professional action have been appropriated. States Chapman:

> As a result of increasing scientific knowledge, growth or profession, and social differentiation, the identification of the ministry with the educated, the privileged, and the powerful has suffered. Today the minister has exclusive possession of sacerdotal practices and theological lore. He is socially selected for his particular church in terms of its specific needs and traditions, the result of social heritage held in common with his parishioners, to lead in worship and the social adjuncts of worship. Aside from these considerations, the minister (and in consequence the church) has lost exclusive possession of the professional field to new professions and specialties.[28]

Although it is well to point out that Herberg had the opportunity to observe and appraise the "come back" of religion since the war, which Chapman had not had when he wrote his paper, this seeming double talk needs further clarification in the meaning of status. This, Chester Barnard provides for us in the distinction of *functional* and *scalar* system of status. Explains Barnard:

> The first kind, which we shall call *functional* systems of status, is that in which status does not depend upon authority and jurisdiction but upon function. The ranks are vertically divided into lateral groups of callings, trades, crafts, metiers, divisions of labor, specializations, and professions. One common characteristic of them all is that the authority of command of one over another is lacking, or is irrelevant at least to the functional status. . . .
>
> In the second kind of status system, which we shall call the *scalar,* status is determined by (1) the relationship of superiority or subordination in a chain of command or formal authority and (2) by jurisdiction. In this kind of status system the primary relationships are customarily conceived as being along vertical lines, of above and below, of superior and subordinate. Status is distinguished by horizontal levels, and integration is by vertical groups, several such groups exemplifying a "pyramid of authority."[29]

What is confusing about many discussions of status in ministerial roles is the fact that the concept of *authority* is equated when this is not warranted. It is possible under a functional system of status for the clergy to relinquish its functions to other professions, make identification with secular society by adopting secular values, fall back upon "sacerdotal practices and theological lore," and still enjoy the rising tide of increased national interest in religion that Herberg reports. In short, the fact that the clergy has lost much of its authority and thereby inherits a marginal position in the contemporary power structure is not invalidated by the temporarily ascending status that has come to the minister on the crest of the swelling tide of religious interest.

Precarious values. The fact that all values are not equal in strength is an obvious but necessary focal point in the understanding of institutions. Values can be identified as precarious when they are poorly defined, ambiguous, vague, lacking in concerted social influence. As the distinctive institutional values become vague there is an increasing dependency upon the individuals who symbolize them and the social relations that build secondary support for the organization. The fact that the distinctively religious values have become increasingly more precarious renders further support to the marginality of the church in contemporary society.

As stated above, there is no doubt but that there has been an upsurge in religious interest in recent years. Unless one pushes on to the deeper and more specific meanings, these religious beliefs are still apt to be precarious. Will Herberg pushes hard at this point when he states:

> We do penetrate a little deeper, it would seem, when we take note of certain curious discrepancies the surveys reveal in the responses people make to questions about their religion. Thus, according to one trustworthy source, 73 per cent said they believed in an afterlife, with God as judge, but "only 5 per cent had any fear, not to say expectation, of going to hell."[30] Indeed, about 80 per cent according to another source, admitted that what they were "most serious about" was not the life after death in which they said they believed, but in trying to live as comfortably in this life as possible.[31] And in their opinion they were not doing so badly even from the point of view of the divine judgment; 91 per cent felt that they could honestly say that they were trying to lead a good life, and 78 per cent felt no hesitation in saying that they more than half measured up to their own standards of goodness, over 50 per cent asserting that they were in fact following the rule of loving one's neighbor as oneself "all the way!"[32] This amazing high valuation that most Americans appear to place on their own virtue would seem to offer a better insight into the basic religion of the American people than any figures as to their formal beliefs can provide, however important in themselves these figures may be.[33]

But perhaps this superficial approach to religious beliefs by the bulk of Americans is understandable when one visits church after church on Sunday morning, as this writer has. He found that sin was being preached about as a "real" matter rather than just a little error or mistake, but the subtle distinctions and specific nature of sin were rarely delineated. Obvious, expected illustrations of sin were common. Likewise, the researcher heard the familiar refrain from pulpits that "Jesus Christ is Lord" and that "the answer is Christ," but seldom did he hear much more than the oft-repeated claim that accepting Jesus Christ as Lord and Savior would create a transformation in individual lives. Other than emphasizing that this would convict one of sin and create a brotherhood of love, the specifics were usually left to God and the individual. It was much more common, for example, to direct the worshipers to prayer. Although there were some exceptions to this pattern, it would seem to this researcher that the poorly defined, vague character of religion as described above would be the expected result of this type of pulpit.[34]

But perhaps the most revealing test of the precarious nature of American religious values is the nature of their influences in contemporary society. Vague and poorly defined values in themselves may actually serve to give an institution the freedom to bear down on a broad range of specific issues because they all fall under the scope of institutional jurisdiction. But what about vague religious values in the church? Do they make it possible for churches to generate concern and action or do they more often result in indifference and escapism? What happens when religious values meet secular values in today's world?

At this point there is a growing feeling of uneasiness even within the church. In the foreword of the 1949 *Yearbook of American Churches,* Dr. Cavert pointed to "the disturbing discrepancy between the numerical size of the church in the United States and its positive influence in the life of our nation."[35] F. Ernest Johnson, past Director of Research and Education for the National Council of Churches, has declared with concern: "When the Christian gospel loses its vital quality of searching, disturbing criticism of accepted ways of living, it is nothing but the ashes of a fire that has burned out."[36] Another plain-talking religious sociologist, who acknowledges "our oppressive moral climate" and describes the nature and possible role of Christian influence has asked some searching questions:

> Why is there such a gulf between the great Protestant tradition of prophetic protest and responsibility and the timidity and inaction of the churches of Jesus Christ? Why so much complacent conformity to the world and so little Christian challenge? Why is there so much talk and so little effective leadership? These demands raise the crucial problem of influence that demands the attention of all earnest Christians.[37]

Is this admission by religious leaders that the church is no humming dynamo of influence merely an intuitive deflection of insight or does there seem to be some evidence for it as a reasonable focal point or concern? In brief, one can reply that though a substantial body of research is wanting, what has been done has supported the churchmen's uneasiness about the situation.

One outstanding case study of the relationship of religion to the economic order was done by Liston Pope in Gaston County, North Carolina. Because an agricultural economy had been superseded by a phenomenal industrial development, this advantageous social context provided an excellent "laboratory" for the observation of religious behavior when religious values come face to face with opposing economic interests. A few direct quotes relate the gist of the outcome:

> This rapid change in economic structure illuminates the whole problem of the relation of religious and economic institutions in Gaston County. When some alteration offers economic advantage, the mills adopt it, and only then. Mill executives mask

their real motives behind the idealism traditionally associated with their role and confirmed in the religious standards prevalent in the county. Ministers who had not been concerned previously with the application of moral judgments to the particular issue in question, suddenly see its new relevance and sanction the change as being for the general welfare of the community. Those ministers who, being closer to the workers, see the more fundamental implications of the proposed change, are circumscribed by their own dependent relation to the mills and can voice no public criticism. The workers, lacking corporate organization or vehicles for self-expression, are confused in their own minds by the public professions of interest in their welfare. Acquiescence of ministers in these professions really helps the mills to make economic changes without opposition, as it abets the confusion of issues in the minds of those most affected.[38]

Another example of research to make a significant breakthrough and nail down some evidence to clarify the contest of specific religious and secular issues is that of Glock and Ringer on church policy and attitudes in the Protestant Episcopal Church.[39] In a national sample involving 234 Episcopal congregations and their ministers, nine specific issues were studied. These social scientists found that on five issues—the United Nations, human rights, conscientious objectors, immigration, and intermarriage—the church had adopted a *committed* position in favor of a given point of view. On the other four issues—the political role of the church, government control, war, and labor—the church's ideology is, or may be interpreted to be, *equivocal*. The striking difference between the two groups is that where the church tends to be partisan, the social issues tend to be *ideological;* and where the church is moderate in its pronouncements, the issues involve the question of *power*—either that relating to distribution of power between classes as in labor and government control, between communities as in war, or within the community as with the political role of the church. In brief, when a real issue of power is at stake, the church is more accommodating than when the matter tends to be ideological.

Still another indication that religious values are precarious stems from the character of the sermons themselves. The element of sales persuasion, designed to convert the pagan, dominated the preaching in most churches. In some churches the "invitation" was given at the close of every sermon and a specifically selected hymn utilized to "move" people to Christ and the church. It would seem that if the church were really at ease about the acceptance of religious values, more sermons would be designed to "refine" and deepen religious understanding. Sunday after Sunday many people sat in the pews listening to sermons that were basically directed to the uncommitted, even though most of the people would have passed that stage long before.

In later chapters we will become aware of other factors that accent the precarious nature of religious values, such as the dependence upon the charismatic character of the religious leader more than upon the personification of the values in the participants themselves, and the undergirding that the purely social relationships provide for the religious institution. Since the above discussion seems to establish the fact, these elaborations will be saved for later.

Resistance to new church buildings. Resistance to new church buildings provides another indication of the marginality of religion in our society. Although this is not a universal phenomenon, it is a prevalent and irksome aspect of church extension on the West Coast. Declared one minister active in the administrative work of his denomination:

> Here on the West Coast there is hardly a new church building that is put up without sizable neighborhood resistance. As it works out, the church usually gets the location; and after the church is built many in the neighborhood become members of the church. But it is unfortunate that this resistance has to be met every time a new site is selected.[40]

Consequences for adult education. These, then, are some of the factors that give assurance to the characterization of the church as a marginal institution in American society. Later on we shall discover that the church attracts most of its people to its educational programs through the institution itself and not to a particular educational aspect of its work. If the church has to first attract its people to a marginal institution and struggle with the consequences of marginality in its internal and external relations, such marginality is bound to have consequences for adult education.

But not only does the adult education program have to attract people to a marginal institution to begin with, the program itself is utilized to counter these secular pressures in society. This is evident in the large expenditure of energy directed to undergird the rationale and value system of the religious institution. This, in part, explains why the adult education program of the church has not been free to develop a broad and inclusive curriculum. The necessities of institutional security demand that the focus be upon the programs that function to support this institutional mandate.

MARGINALITY AND ORGANIZATIONAL CHARACTER

The marginality of a religious institution is also accented when the character of that particular institution is not supported by the cultural base on which it finds itself. When institutional accommodation to the cultural base is blocked and retarded because of institutional rigidities, the ability of that institution to recruit members and gain support is drastically curtailed and its marginality accented.

Two recent organizational studies render good illustrations of this phenomenon. Sheldon L. Messinger has described the Townsend Movement as an organization born of the 1930's with a mission to promote national pensions for the aged as a mechanism for alleviating or preventing economic dislocation.[41] When the economic disaster moved into "boom" times, the membership of the movement dropped drastically (between 1936 and 1951 there was a 97 per cent decrease), and a corresponding change of organizational character began to be evident in (1) tendencies to deflect from the original mission, (2) tendencies toward salesmanship to provide for a financial base, and (3) tendencies to "pure" recreation as the "real" business of the meetings. In short, the Townsend Movement was able to make something of a comeback when it made a shift in organizational character more in keeping with the needs and interests of the cultural base.

On the other hand, Joseph Gusfield has given us a good study of the Woman's Christian Temperance Union, in which there has been no gradual modification in the structure and ideology of the movement.[42] Instead of new activities comparable to the Townsend Movement's devices to perpetuate the organization's membership, income, and power, the W.C.T.U. has not acted to preserve organizational values at the expense of past doctrine. As a consequence this moral reform movement, which drew recruits from a socially dominant group satisfied with the major outlines of the social structure, has shifted to the marginal position of a "moralizer-in-retreat"[43] and is now open to ridicule and censure from the new middle class. States Gusfield:

> Today the W.C.T.U. is an organization in retreat. Contrary to the expectations of theories of institutionalization, the movement has not acted to preserve the organizational values at the expense of past doctrine. In adhering to less popular positions, it has played the role of the sect and widened the gap between W.C.T.U. membership and middle-class respectability. Analysis of social composition in this stage indicates that the movement is today less upper middle class in composition than in earlier periods, and more lower middle and lower class in composition. In this respect, as well as in the changing drinking norms of the upper middle classes, the split within American Protestant middle classes has widened.[44]

Just as the W.C.T.U. member often finds herself open to ridicule and censure, the local church member may experience the same sort of uncomfortable situation. Russell Dynes has shown that in the church-sect typology "churchness is asso-

ciated with high socioeconomic status and, consequently, sectness is associated with low socioeconomic status."[45] Likewise,
Thomas Ford Hoult has found that in Los Angeles local
churches and denominations tend to be located in areas which
match the socioeconomic characteristics of the membership.[46]

In the San Francisco Bay Area this general phenomenon is
also observable, although there are certain interesting discrepancies. For example, the Baptist and Presbyterian churches
in the downtown setting both demonstrated their commitment
to minister to the neighborhood around the church, which
was of a lower socioeconomic level than the church members.
Yet the First Presbyterian Church had made no appreciable
dent with this objective at the time of this study, while First
Baptist Church had made some marked progress in integrating
not only the lower socioeconomic levels but also Japanese,
Chinese, Negro, and, to a limited extent, American Indian
ethnic groups. On the other hand, the Baptists had been sur-
passed in the suburbs where higher socioeconomic levels pre-
dominate. The mean membership figure for Baptist churches
here is only 263[47] as compared to the mean membership figure
of 817[48] for the Presbyterians. Although the following chapters
deal more extensively with this phenomenon, we can acknowledge here that organizational character may tend toward marginality with one cultural base while enjoying greater acceptance in another. Likewise, it is also possible for a church to
accommodate to its cultural base over a period of time and
win recruits from its environment, whereas this would have
been unlikely before.

MARGINALITY AND INTERNAL STRUCTURE

Not only is marginality one of the widespread problems of
the church in contemporary society, but the educational program of the church is characterized by widespread marginality
within the religious institution. Any appraisal of adult education in the church must take into account the organizational
pressures under which the adult program of the church must

exist, day in and day out. Throughout the rest of this chapter the reader will gain appreciation of the dependence of religious adult education upon the directives of the parent institution. Adult education in the church has very little status of its own except when it serves to help the parent institution meet its problems and satisfy its needs.

This discourse now turns to some of the indices of marginality in educational phases of church work gathered from a variety of sources.

Worship vs. educational activities. Some will undoubtedly rebel at the thought of setting educational activities over against worship activities, because much has been said in the literature of the church about the integration of these two functions in particular church programs and the interrelationship of these two phases within the life of the church. A few clergymen have undoubtedly integrated these two phases of religious expression in such a fashion that integrity results. But we shall observe that for many clergymen and laymen alike there are serious discrepancies between theological rationale and actual behavior.

Actually the laity had no difficulty whatever with this polarity. When questions concerning worship and education were juxtaposed, the immediate response to the term "worship" was the main Sunday morning worship service in the sanctuary. The immediate response to the term "education" was Sunday church school. Thus we have striking evidence that the theological rationale had not effectively reached the laity. Consequently this polarity presented no significant theological problem for sociological research.

In the questionnaire used with group leaders, all of whom had some responsibility for educational activities in their groups, these leaders rated Sunday morning worship above both Sunday church school for children and educational groups for adults (although an evening worship service rated lowest of all). Furthermore it is significant to note that the educational emphasis is secondary to the worship emphasis in

TABLE 1

CHURCH ACTIVITIES IN ORDER OF IMPORTANCE

Activity	Raw Score	Rank
Sunday morning worship services	92	1
Sunday school for children	140	2
Educational groups for adults	241	3
Mission programs at home	277	4
Mission programs overseas	280	5
Evening worship services	320	6

Source: Seventy-four adult group leaders responding to a questionnaire in nine East Bay churches.

TABLE 2

ADULT GROUP ACTIVITIES IN ORDER OF IMPORTANCE

Activity	Raw Score	Rank
Worship	125	1
Education	164	2
Service projects	186	3
Social activities	203	4

Source: Seventy-four adult group leaders responding to a questionnaire in nine East Bay churches.

the groups themselves. Tables 1 and 2, respectively, were responses to questionnaire items that asked the respondents to rank (number 1 as most important, number 2 as next in importance, etc.) various church activities.

Not only was this the point of view of the lay leaders responsible for adult education in the church, but it also characterized without exception the position of the clergy. In interview after interview with clergymen in various staff positions, the researcher was told that the Sunday morning worship service was the most important single activity in the life of the church. Frequently the question was asked: "Suppose that you had only one service on Sunday and a group of adults wanted to meet at that hour for study purposes. What chance would there be for this to materialize?" Invariably the respondents answered that there would be little if any chance for this to take place. Such a proposition would not only attract the restraining hand of the clergy but would also have the opposition of the active laity.

Moreover, the type of adult education that goes on in the church is mainly a low-pressure variety. Educational objectives have to be shared with social activities and service projects designed to further the local or benevolent objectives of the church. Although there has been some attempt at accreditation (as in the case of leadership education), it has meant little in the boosting of standards or motivation. Adult group participants with sufficient background to appraise educational standards most frequently characterized the standards of their groups as vague and indefinite.

In contrast to this the standards for worship services are much higher in comparison, and every clergyman can talk at length about the rationale for his type of worship service. During the course of this research, adjustments were made in the order of several church services either because the existing order of worship did not fit the clerical rationale or because the congregation was not satisfied at one point or another. It was also a frequent item for discussion at committee and "official board" meetings.

In short, the worship experience in the sanctuary on Sunday morning is seen to be the most meaningful relationship that a man can have with God, and the values of the educational experience are definitely not considered equal to those of the worship service. Worship is considered the "hub" of the church program and is accepted as such by the clergy and the laity alike.

Furthermore, even the adult group leaders themselves look upon the educational program of the church as a marginal activity and their standards as vague. A low-pressure type of education must be shared with many other functions in each adult group.

"Line" and "staff" relationships. The staff relationships in the religious institution are a particularly rich source of information about the marginality of the educational program of the church. In every large-scale organization two vertical groupings of officeholders seem to emerge: (1) the *line* organization, which has exclusive authority over the process of integrating the various activities of the organization in relation to institutional purpose; and (2) the *staff* organization, which functions to serve the institution in some special capacity. As Dalton[49] has pointed out, there are invariably tensions in staff and line relationships. The religious organization is not immune to this common phenomenon in social organizations.

Protestantism, whether it is thought of as under an episcopal form of church government or under the more autonomous congregational polity, has been traditionally a "parish ministry." In a widely dispersed institution (churches must be built where the people live), the central figure in the institution is the local church pastor who administrates a local church. In every denomination there is a grouping of local churches into some collective "association" (although in theory the relationship to the association is variously defined) and further collective bodies on higher levels until something like the traditional pyramid takes form. At each level there is an administrative officer who integrates the work of the denomination at that level. From the local parish on up, these administrative officials, who are charged with the responsibility of integrating the work of the church, should be thought of as line officers, and those who serve the organization in some special capacity, as staff.

Through the years the ministers who have been sent out from theological seminaries have been trained to be line officers at the local parish level. Every minister is expected to be capable of serving in the pastoral ministry if need be. If and when a specialized ministry is terminated, it is expected that the ministerial specialist will be willing and capable of taking an assignment or "call" as a pastor of a local church. However, when and if he should step back into the line, it is usually at a lower level of advancement than those men who have stayed in the line.[50]

Perhaps the best indication of the marginality of the minister of Christian education is the salary differential. The minister of education is invariably the "low man on the totem pole." A typical spread of monetary rewards is illustrated here in the 1959 budget of First Baptist Church.

Pastor	
Salary	$7,800
Housing	1,800
Car allowance	1,200
	10,800
Associate Pastor	
Salary	4,560
Housing	1,200
Car allowance	1,200
	6,960
Minister of Music	
Salary	5,100
Car allowance	900
	6,000
Minister of Education	
Salary	3,400
Housing	1,200
Car allowance	1,200
	5,880

The marginality of the minister of education is also indicated by the order in which staff is added to a growing church. During the course of this research, First Methodist Church hired a minister of education. This church already had a pastor, associate pastor, and minister of music on a full-time basis before the minister of education was hired. Previous to this event the educational ministry was under the leadership of part-time seminary students, active laymen, and the part-time attention of the associate minister. In short, it was not until three full-time ministers had been provided that the church added a full-time minister of education.

Likewise in the smaller churches the educational work is among the first things that are delegated to active laymen or seminary students. In sharp contrast to this the pulpit leadership is one of the most zealously guarded and protected of all church leadership functions.

Noteworthy is the fact that in no church (to the researcher's knowledge) is the minister of education looked upon as the major administrator or designer of policy in the local church. The pulpit man is always associated with this function. Although there is often much talk about the fine "team" spirit in the staff, the stratification is always clear and distinct if one will take the time to find the indices.

A further factor about the staff relationship is that a staff position with responsibilities in education is frequently seen as a place of beginning in one's ministerial career. Staff men in the churches of this study frequently referred to the fact that one of the most rewarding aspects of their position was the fact that they could gain valuable experience under a top-notch administrator and see how "big" churches did things. When the researcher asked about future plans he found only one minister of education who was not thinking about "a church of his own" in the future.

Incidentally, the position of minister of education is also seen as a good spot for transferring from one denomination to another. Since there is less competition for these positions, an outsider can enter a denomination without "bumping" the "legitimate" sons of the denomination.

This leads us to the further observation that good candidates for the position of minister of education are difficult to find. Because churches see this position as marginal and make no significant adjustments in salary for tenure that would be commensurate with "climbing the ladder" to more significant pulpits, it is only the unusually dedicated man who doesn't weary of pulling his family through a "financial knothole" while his peers take on the more remunerative positions. One clergyman, lamenting the difficulty of filling staff positions, complained:

> It is next to impossible to find a really good minister of education today. When a good man comes along, he can have his pick of opportunities. We haven't limited our search for an M.C.E. to our own denomination because one can seldom be found when you need him. This church has had to go to other denominations to get adequate leadership.[51]

It appears evident that when staff relationships are analyzed the person who has responsibility for the educational program of the church is in a markedly marginal position. Certainly an organization that perpetuates this kind of incentive and stratification pattern, in spite of recognized difficulties involved in finding adequate leadership, does not place its educational program very high in its esteem.

Financial indices. A further indication that the educational program of the church "knows its place" is that the major offerings of the parishioners are rendered through the Sunday morning worship service. Throughout the church school, token offerings are given (usually in the form of coins), and the major portion of the parishioners' financial response is reserved for the "appropriate" Sunday morning worship service. Here they are dedicated in a very sober and dignified act of worship that is in marked contrast to the passing of the basket which is the custom in most adult classes.

The widespread adoption of the "unified budget plan," in which the church school gives up its offerings to the church treasury and subjects its budget to the church's general fiscal policy, further reveals the place of the educational program.

Education as a means to organizational ends. A further indication of educational marginality is the way that the educational work of the church is used to further organizational objectives. In Chapter I we saw the character of the educational program vary with the needs and problems of the church in each era. The same characteristic is true of the religious education in the contemporary church: it is utilized in the process of meeting institutional problems and needs.

One of the ongoing needs of a religious institution is members, and therefore evangelism is frequently thought of as the "basic work of the church." It is not surprising then to find an emphasis on evangelism in the teaching ministry of the church. This abiding theme is illustrated in a leaflet put out by the Department of General Church School Work of The Methodist Church:

> By evangelism we mean the winning of people to Christ and to membership in the church. . . . Evangelism in the church school is getting persons to commit their lives to Christ as Savior and to join the church.
>
> Viewed from this angle, evangelism is an integral part of Christian education. It deals with commitment and loyalty to Christ. With some individuals the consciousness of commitment may come gradually as a product of many decisions in specific situations to follow Christ. It may be a process of natural growth that comes to fruition in a declaration of loyalty to Christ. These decisions should climax in public commitment and dramatic heart-warming experience. The process whereby the individual is led to make decisions to follow Christ in specific is educational. The fact that it has led to commitment is evangelistic. It is the teacher's job to lead persons in making the decision for Christ, acknowledged publicly through word and deed. . . .
>
> The record shows that the church school has a great opportunity as an evangelistic agency. The ration of approximately six out of every ten additions to the church coming through the church school persists year after year and indicates the crucial importance of the church school in the evangelistic work of the church.[52]

Not only does the religious institution need committed members but it also needs committed pocketbooks. Here again, when organizational needs have to be met, it is natural that the educational program of the church would reflect this need. In discussing "Standard V–A" in the committee handbook on missionary and stewardship education, the following specific directions are given:

(1) *The World Fellowship Offering.* Sunday, October 4, 1959, is World Fellowship Offering Sunday. The theme for this offering is "Expanding Christian Ties in Thailand." . . .

Children, youth, and adults will give generously if they can feel close to the Thai people. Ask teachers to use materials in such a way as to make Thailand "live" for their class members. . . .

(2) *The America for Christ Offering.* This is the second of the American Baptist missions presentations. Like the first, it involves three Sundays—two leading up to the offering, and the following Sunday. The dates will be February 14, 21, and 28, 1960. Here again, the Chairman and the Committee on Missionary and Stewardship Education will want to see that the available resources are brought to the attention of the age group chairman and that appropriate plans are made.

It is well to keep in mind that these annual offerings go to make up the bread-and-butter budget of the national agencies. They are not "extra." On three successive Sundays in the fall, the winter, and the spring you have an opportunity to do an effective job of missionary education throughout the Sunday church school. . . .

(3) *The Children's Day Offering.* This helps to expand the evangelistic Winning the Children for Christ Program. A special service interpreting the purpose of the offering is planned for use in the youth and adult departments on the Sunday preceding Children's Day, or on Children's Day itself. June 12 is the date for 1960. Interpretive materials should reach the pastor, the Sunday church school superintendent, and the Chairman of Children's Work by April 1.[53]

As we see, it becomes second nature for churchmen to think of the educational program of the church as a means to meet the particular needs and problems of the religious institution. Religious educators have long since accepted this function and it has become a natural aspect of their day-to-day work. It is not our purpose to criticize this characteristic but merely to point out that whenever the educational program shifts in emphasis from one objective to another, as is frequently the case in order to support more effectively some organizational need, it takes on the marginal characteristic of serving purposes by external mandate rather than by internal direction.

Goal diffusion. As we have just seen, certain operating pressures of the religious institution inevitably have their influence upon the educational program of the church. In brief, what is taking place is that the educational program of the church is adapting to the wishes and needs of the organization as a whole rather than building an identity of its own and finding an internal direction within itself. This pattern of dependency can take place in religious education because of the absence of any restrictive goals and objectives. Instead, the goals are ambiguous and thereby allow external decisions the freedom of shaping educational character.

The following are typical of the many statements of purpose that one will find as a preface to handbooks and leaflets describing church groups:

> The purpose of this organization shall be to promote the Kingdom of God world-wide by encouraging Presbyterian men to serve Jesus Christ in the work of the church, and to follow him in the vocations of the common life. Further, to encourage Presbyterian men to organize themselves for the following purposes:
>
> a. To sustain more adequately and to enlarge the work of the local church in the community.
> b. To take an active part in the meetings and work of presbytery, synod, and General Assembly.
> c. To help and encourage the local church in fulfilling its commitments and responsibilities to the world-wide mission of the church.[54]
>
> The ship is launched to promote such interest as shall help all shipmates to have a safe voyage with happy homes and no

shipwrecks; to carry a cargo of service to the church and community; and to provide happy decks with social contacts and
fellowship of a Christian nature.[55]

The purpose of this Council is to unite Baptist women in their
devotion to their Lord and Savior, Jesus Christ, through a
program that will cultivate a missionary spirit and a definite
commitment to active participation in attaining the objectives
of the American Baptist Convention.[56]

Such statements reflect considerable ambiguity of purpose
in the groups that promote adult education in the church.
It isn't difficult to see that such statements do not constitute
many *specific* directives for group planning, nor do they constitute any real barriers to program alterations. Goals can
shape decisions when they become specific and are invested
with value over a long period of time. However this is not
characteristic of adult groups within the church. Without
such internal directives it is easy to see how the program and
inevitably the character of an adult group changes with the
needs and problems of the parent institution.

ADULT EDUCATION AND MARGINALITY

In summary we can acknowledge that *the church itself is in
a marginal position in American society*. Through the separation of church and state the church has built no vested interest in government from which it could speak with authority
and power. Instead, religion in America has spawned into a
proliferation of separate religious organizations that fragment
the religious enterprise into a number of un-co-ordinated units.
Although the ecumenical movement has tended to direct
some energies toward unity, the great bulk of the religious
effort is turned inward toward the sustaining of individual
local churches and individual denominations. Through the
years institutionalization has built up rigidities in denominational structures that now serve as barriers to co-operative
enterprises, such as might easily materialize in the area of
adult education. In its fragmentation the church is no match

for the tremendous power of social collectives, and this is indicated by the precarious nature of religious values in contemporary society. To be sure, the marginality of the religious enterprise does not blanket all institutions equally but varies somewhat with organizational character and the cultural base of which we shall have more to say.

Although the marginality of the parent institution makes for weaker organizational structures and directs energies into specific channels, *the position of dependency, which describes educational activities within the church, further limits the scope and nature of adult education.* Education is seen to be of lesser value than worship activities, and the marginality is further accented by staff relationships and financial indices. In such a position education is frequently utilized as a means to meeting organizational ends. It becomes second nature for religious leaders to think of building numerical and financial strength through educational endeavors, and adult education is frequently directed toward these objectives.

All this is made possible within the educational life of the church because of *the diffuse goals which are set before the educational enterprise.* Diffuse goals are not likely to control decision-making. Therefore, when organizational problems rear their heads, the educational phase of church work is enlisted to meet the situation. Since organizational needs rule the day it shall not be surprising to find in succeeding chapters that much of adult education in the church serves to support institutional survival and security. Although the elements abstracted in this chapter do not determine all facets of organizational behavior or the character of education in the church, they throw considerable weight in that direction.

Chapter III

SOCIAL SELECTIVITY IN
ADULT EDUCATION

CAREFUL OBSERVERS of American society have recognized that the religious institution reflects the characteristics of social stratification that describe the surrounding environment.[1] In spite of the fact that the church has thrown wide its doors with announcements, from the pulpit and in national convocations, of its intentions to be an inclusive fellowship, it is plain that the general population continue to be selective in their religious affiliation. Denominations and local churches, therefore, tend to minister to narrowly stratified segments of the total community in spite of their avowed "open door" policy. As a result of this phenomenon, adult education in the church has a selective clientele. In this chapter we shall take a look at the process of social selectivity and draw some implications for adult education under the sponsorship of the church.

SOCIAL STRATIFICATION AND DENOMINATIONS

That Protestantism in America is class- and sometimes caste-stratified can be seen in the differences between the members of selected Protestant denominations. A survey conducted by the American Institute of Public Opinion in 1945–1946 is one of the most widely cited studies that document this phenome-

non. The social class levels of the twelve thousand inter-
viewees are tabulated in Table 3. Although this study is now
somewhat dated and undoubtedly biased throughout in an
upward direction, the stratification indicated would probably
be substantially the same today. In general, the Table indicates that Congregational, Episcopalian, and Presbyterian denominations may be regarded as relatively higher in the stratification system than Baptist, Lutheran, and Methodist denominations. Small denominations have an even higher percentage
of lower-class members. Goldschmidt[2] found that 84 per cent
of the Pentecostals in part of California were unskilled laborers, compared with 19 per cent for the Assembly of God,
15 per cent for the Baptists, and 1 per cent for the Congrega-
tionalists. Similarly, Pope[3] and Boisen[4] have found in their
field studies that these movements start among the very poor,
although they may later move up the social ladder.

A further documentation of denominational stratification
is of another sort. H. Richard Niebuhr, convinced that a
purely theological explanation of denominational differences

TABLE 3

COMPOSITION OF SELECTED PROTESTANT DENOMINATIONS BY
SOCIAL CLASS LEVEL, UNITED STATES, 1945–1946

| Denomination | Class Levels by Percentages[a] | | |
	Upper Class	Middle Class	Lower Class
Congregational	24	43	33
Episcopalian	24	34	42
Presbyterian	22	40	35
Methodist	13	35	52
Lutheran	11	36	53
Baptist	8	24	68

Source: American Institute of Public Opinion poll, as reported in Jessie
Barnard, *American Community Behavior* (The Dryden Press, 1949), p. 198.

[a] These percentages seem realistic for comparative purposes only, since
they appear to be consistently biased in an upward direction.

was artificial and limited, turned to history and sociology for a more satisfactory account. His *Social Sources of Denominationalism*[5] emphasizes social class, race immigration (nationalism), and sectionalism as variables of denominational differentiation on the American scene.

For example, in characterizing the Baptist traditions there is a tracing of present-day Baptists from the religiously disinherited English Separatist movement that bridged the Atlantic and grew among the lower economic classes on the frontier of New England at the time of the Great Awakening (1734–1735) and afterward. Spreading with great success on the new frontier of the 1800's in Kentucky and Tennessee, where the economic and cultural conditions of the frontier demanded an emotional fervor, the movement accommodated itself to the conditions of the frontier as it moved westward and into the southland with an appeal to emotions, lay preaching, and the ordination of clergymen without theological training. Thus the Baptists today have a heritage that is rooted among the lower economic levels of society with many sect-type traditions. It is such traditions that give one an appreciation and an explanation for the stratifying characteristics of present-day denominations. The historical, sociological, and theological watersheds of other ages are not unrelated to contemporary religious denominations.

SOCIAL STRATIFICATION AND COMMUNITIES

Another approach to the study of social stratification in Protestant denominations is through community studies. In fact, these studies usually yield much more precise information concerning religion and the class structure than opinion polls, in spite of the fact that they were not primarily written for the purpose of describing the characteristics of social stratification in churches.

From a growing number of such studies, one has been arbitrarily selected for brief comment. It is not necessarily "typical" or "average"—whatever those terms mean to the reader—

but it does seem to bring out the recurring characteristic of selective participation.

At the southern end of the Great Central Valley of California is the little unincorporated town of Wasco with about 4,000 persons.[6] The people are native whites who have come to California from the Middle West. Many of them are of German descent. Besides the native whites, Mexicans (many of whom have been there as long as the whites) and Negroes (who colonized in Wasco shortly after the First World War) are represented in the local population. The industrialization of agriculture that is so typical of California is characteristic of Wasco. Since mechanization and industrialization are fast dominating the rural scene in America, this setting provides an appropriate location for the study of religious characteristics.

In this study on Wasco, Walter Goldschmidt has a chapter on "Social Status and Religious Life." He states:

The church—at least the Protestant Church—is as much a social institution as it is a religious one. When a resident decides to belong to a church, and when he selects the denomination to which he will adhere, he makes a fundamental social choice which will affect his associates and his social behavior for the duration of his residence. And his choice is as much influenced by social considerations as by religious ones.[7]

Farther on he comments:

There is another aspect to the appeals of the several churches —that of belonging to a group of kindred spirits. This is a potent factor in the selection of members on a class basis. People like to "be with their own kind" when being with others means remaining always on the peripheries of participation. Yet people do not want to associate with people who are "beneath them." These social aspects have led to class segregation and such segregation is a specific denial of the basic tenents of Christian philosophy. The church members deny any policy of exclusion, and can document their denial with examples. Yet the exclusion

is of such an insidious nature that it is felt at both ends, and
there is a tacit recognition that certain churches are for certain
people, and this is sometimes given overt expression.[8]

The author sizes up the churches of the area in three separate groups: the elite church of the community, the churches
of "substance," and the revivalistic churches, which he divides
into those which have developed more settled patterns and
those with more pronounced "sectness." After describing the
elite church, which is made up of "select patrons of middle-
class well-being," he describes the middle group, not only
characterizing this group, but also providing us with some
grasp of what is above and below.

Coming down but half a step, we may place two or three congregations on a social level, the differences between them not
being those of social status. Comfortable, unelaborate structures, completely adequate in size to meet the requirements of
the congregation, house the religious services. The sermons are
more fervid, the spirit is less subdued, and the lay participation
is more spontaneous. Correlatively the congregation is more active, the pews are more nearly filled each week, revivalistic meetings are undertaken, and the emotional appeal of Protestantism
more manifest.

These congregations endeavor to bring together persons from
widely different walks of life. Their success has not been great
among the outsider group, yet they are not entirely without
representation from farm laborers. The influence of more factors upon church affiliation is illustrated by the case of a person
of Mexican ancestry who has succeeded in becoming identified
with the nuclear group in the community. This shift not only
involved acquiring a white-collar job and marriage outside the
Mexican group but also a rejection of the Catholic Church, to
which most Mexicans belong, in favor of the Protestant congregation.[9]

Table 4 indicates the occupational characteristics of the
churches and reports that one church has 50 per cent of its

TABLE 4

OCCUPATIONAL CHARACTERISTICS OF CHURCH MEMBERS IN WASCO, CALIFORNIA[a]

Occupation class	Congregational	Methodist	Baptist	Catholic	Christian Science	Seventh-Day Adventist	Nazarene	Assembly of God	Church of Christ	Schismatic Pentecost	All
A. Professionals, managers, and proprietors	50	16	16	16	82	15	11	0	0	0	18
B. Farm operators	20	26	29	22	9	40	22	30	22	0	24
C. Clerical workers	11	14	12	14	9	3	0	10	3	1	9
D. Skilled laborers	18	41	28	26	0	37	45	40	36	17	30
E. Unskilled laborers	1	3	15	22	0	5	22	20	39	82	19
Total	100	100	100	100	100	100	100	100	100	100	100

Source: Walter Goldschmidt, *As You Sow* (The Free Press of Glencoe, 1947), p. 136.
[a] Data from membership rolls and by interview. The number of members of each church for whom occupation was determined, were in order named: 153, 154, 180, 93, 11, 59, 72, 60, and 72.

membership among the professionals, managers, and proprietors and that the traditionally sect-type churches have a disproportionally high number of skilled and unskilled laborers. The Baptist and Roman Catholic churches, however, revealed a fairly even spread of social classes not far from the picture of the population as a whole. Does this mean that these churches necessarily disqualify our general observation? I think not.

When churches are "on the move" they may have attracted a lower social class in the past, but now they are changing as succeeding generations change. As the sons and daughters of immigrant parents begin to climb the social ladder and go off to school to prepare for white-collar occupations and as the clergy is introduced to more and more formal education, a denomination will change in order to hold and attract more persons on these social levels. In the meantime it has not outgrown its past and some "old-timers" may still be around. Such a church does not exist without considerable internal tension. Such tension was revealed in the Wasco report.

One woman who had been invited to the Baptist Church went to the Pentecostal Church instead and explained: "We belonged to the Baptist back home. To tell the truth, I don't like the Baptist Church here because they are a different class of people, and I'd rather stay around my own class. I don't like all the ways they believe in the Pentecostal Church though."[10] Another woman made the following observation: "The children go to the Pentecostal Sunday school. We were Baptist back home, but we don't go to any church out here. We don't have the clothes. Back home there were little old meetings and you could go any old way. When you're just raised up among folks it's different from the way it is here."[11] One of the ministers indicated his awareness of the social consciousness when he reported:

> It is true that many of these people have left their religion behind them. I have frequently tried to get them into the church,

but they don't seem interested. Many of them join the Pentecostal Church. I have never thought of just why that might be, but many of them have pretty tough sledding, and also the emotional nature of the church appeals to them. The Baptist Church in the region they come from is more emotional too. Most of the people I have talked to say they don't feel well enough off. We just inducted a couple of agricultural laborers who have just come from Oklahoma. They have quite poor clothes, but they don't seem to mind.[12]

SOCIAL STRATIFICATION IN THE BAY AREA

Since most of the studies of social stratification have been in churches of rural or quite settled communities, questions concerning metropolitan areas have been more speculative. Do churches in urban areas provide the same opportunities for individuals to associate with "their kind," or does the highly mobile, ever-changing, impersonal character of the urban population blur these distinctions? Some clues supporting social stratification as a persistent phenomenon in the urban communities have been provided by such works as Louis Bultena's study[13] of church membership and attendance in Madison, Wisconsin, and Russell Dynes's study[14] of the sect-church typology in Columbus, Ohio, but particular churches were not identified as such. It was partially to provide an answer to this question that the adult group participants of nine Bay Area churches were surveyed.

Geographical distribution. A further clue to the fact that churches in urban areas recruit a selective social base is indicated by the distances that people travel to get to the "right" church. Table 5 indicates that the "downtown" churches (First Presbyterian, First Methodist, and First Baptist) are the best examples of wide geographical dispersion. But even the so-called "neighborhood" churches of the intermediate area (Second Presbyterian, Second Methodist, and Second Baptist) and the suburban area (Third Presbyterian, Third Methodist, and Third Baptist) were pulling the bulk of their people from

TABLE 5

DISTANCE FROM CHURCH OF ADULT GROUP PARTICIPANTS IN NINE BAY AREA CHURCHES

Distance from Church (Miles)	First Baptist	Second Baptist	Third Baptist	First Methodist	Second Methodist	Third Methodist	First Presbyterian	Second Presbyterian	Third Presbyterian
¼	2	5	14	2	12	3	7	16	2
½	1	10	12	2	2	5	8	11	6
¾	3	11	8	4	2	8	10	5	3
1–2	39	29	17	14	24	41	71	27	14
3–5	78	18	24	32	13	36	109	14	43
6–10	33	3	7	4	6	4	55	3	5
over 10	14	2	0	4	9	1	32	0	0
Total	170	78	82	62	68	100	292	76	73

Source: Data from 1,001 questionnaire respondents in nine Bay Area churches.

distances of one to five miles. Statistics such as these, as well as the sight of large numbers of automobiles that spill out and beyond the church parking facilities, indicate that church members are climbing into their automobiles on Sunday morning and driving to a church of their choice rather than walking to the nearest Protestant church in the neighborhood.

Variables of social stratification. Income, occupation, and education are considered three of the most reliable indices of class affiliation. Although most of the churches have some representation in each rubric, some striking comparisons can be made. For example, in Table 6 it can be seen that the much higher family incomes of Third Presbyterian (where 53.4 per cent of the families have incomes of $10,000 or more) and First Presbyterian compare in striking fashion to Second Methodist, Second Presbyterian, and Second Baptist. Likewise the white-collar occupations (Table 7) in Third Presbyterian, First Presbyterian, and Third Methodist stand in striking contrast to the blue collar occupations of Second Methodist, Second Baptist, Second Presbyterian, and Third Baptist. Although every church had a sizable group of people who had made an attempt at formal education beyond grade school, Table 8 indicates that Third Presbyterian and First Presbyterian had considerably more members singing the songs of their alma mater.

It would therefore appear that urban churches also have pronounced patterns of social stratification. This is never an absolute matter, for social conditions and participants are never static. Nor do we have analytical procedures available in social research to make absolute characterizations. Nevertheless, at least eight of these churches (First Baptist will be discussed below) reflected the patterns of social stratification of the metropolitan community of which they were a part in the above three variables, and selectively recruited their participants whether the churches were aware of it or not.

Church-sect scale. The church-sect typology can also be used as an index of social stratification in religious institutions when it is utilized in the form of a scale as supplied by Russell R. Dynes.[15] Dynes reduced the theoretical constructs of church and sect as identified by Liston Pope[16] to six basic statements and then developed a scale of twenty-four attitudes that he has offered as an empirical measurement of this institutional typology. Dynes found that "churchness is associated with high socioeconomic status, and, conversely, that sectness is associated with low socioeconomic status."[17] Table 9 records the church-sect scores of the adult group participants in the nine Bay Area churches of this study. Although the nine churches did not take in the extremes of church and sect (just three major denominations were included), a range of nineteen points reflects considerable differentiation between churches. Once again First Presbyterian and Third Presbyterian reflect the higher socioeconomic stratification and Second Methodist and Second Presbyterian reflect low socioeconomic stratification.

TABLE 6

ANNUAL FAMILY INCOME OF ADULT GROUP PARTICIPANTS IN NINE BAY AREA CHURCHES BY PERCENTAGES

Annual Family Income	First Baptist	Second Baptist	Third Baptist	First Methodist	Second Methodist	Third Methodist	First Presbyterian	Second Presbyterian	Third Presbyterian	All Churches
Under $2,000	9.4	3.8	7.3	8.1	11.8	0.0	3.1	7.9	0.0	5.3
$2,000 to $2,999	7.6	2.6	2.4	4.8	22.1	3.0	1.7	5.3	0.0	4.7
$3,000 to $3,999	12.9	17.8	9.8	8.1	17.7	4.0	6.2	7.9	0.0	8.9
$4,000 to $4,999	11.8	10.2	7.3	19.0	20.6	8.0	9.9	6.6	2.7	10.4
$5,000 to $5,999	11.8	19.2	15.9	11.3	11.8	13.0	8.9	30.3	2.7	12.7
$6,000 to $6,999	9.4	14.1	14.6	17.7	8.8	18.0	9.9	23.7	12.3	13.0
$7,000 to $7,999	8.2	11.5	13.4	9.7	3.0	18.0	12.0	6.6	9.1	10.7
$8,000 to $8,999	5.9	10.2	13.4	8.1	4.4	8.0	9.9	5.3	15.1	8.8
$9,000 to $9,999	9.4	2.6	3.7	4.8	0.0	11.0	8.6	5.3	4.1	6.7
$10,000 or more	13.5	7.7	12.2	8.1	0.0	17.0	29.5	2.6	53.4	18.9
All Groups[a]	100.8	99.7	100.0	99.7	100.2	100.0	99.7	101.5	99.4	100.1

Source: Data from 1,001 questionnaire respondents divided among the churches in the order named: 170, 78, 82, 62, 68, 100, 292, 76, 73.

[a] Details do not always add to 100% because of rounding.

TABLE 7

Occupations of Adult Group Participations in Nine Bay Area Churches by Percentages

Occupational Categories	First Baptist	Second Baptist	Third Baptist	First Methodist	Second Methodist	Third Methodist	First Presbyterian	Second Presbyterian	Third Presbyterian	All Churches
Professional, technical, and kindred workers	30.0	9.0	14.6	16.3	10.3	33.0	38.0	11.8	39.7	26.9
Managers, officials, and proprietors	11.2	11.5	19.5	21.0	3.0	22.0	21.2	9.2	34.2	17.5
Sales workers	9.4	3.8	8.5	16.3	5.9	13.0	7.2	10.5	20.5	9.7
Craftsmen, foremen, and kindred workers	13.6	43.6	31.7	6.5	11.8	15.0	9.2	26.3	1.4	15.8
Clerical and kindred workers	7.6	11.5	4.9	8.1	14.7	1.0	4.8	9.2	1.4	6.4
Operatives and kindred workers	2.4	5.1	3.7	1.6	10.3	4.0	0.0	13.2	0.0	3.4
Service workers and laborers	2.4	5.1	2.5	3.2	17.7	3.0	1.0	10.5	1.4	3.9
Others and retired	23.5	10.2	14.6	27.4	26.5	9.0	18.1	9.2	1.4	16.5
All Groups[a]	100.1	99.8	99.9	100.4	100.2	100.0	99.5	99.9	100.0	100.1

Source: Data from 1,001 questionnaire respondents divided among the churches in the order named: 170, 78, 82, 62, 68, 100, 292, 76, 73.

a Details do not always add to 100% because of rounding.

TABLE 8

Formal Education of Adult Group Participants in Nine Bay Area Churches by Percentages

Amount of Formal Education	First Baptist	Second Baptist	Third Baptist	First Methodist	Second Methodist	Third Methodist	First Presbyterian	Second Presbyterian	Third Presbyterian	All Churches
Grade school or less	5.9	3.8	2.4	1.6	4.4	4.0	1.7	11.8	1.4	3.8
Some high school	9.4	16.7	9.8	4.8	11.8	2.0	6.5	9.2	0.0	7.6
High school graduate	17.7	55.1	39.0	22.6	27.9	28.0	15.4	47.4	13.7	25.7
Some college	34.1	15.4	34.1	41.9	44.1	37.0	28.5	18.4	21.9	30.4
College graduate	12.4	3.8	9.8	12.9	5.9	17.0	27.4	10.5	38.4	17.7
Some graduate work	10.0	1.3	1.2	9.7	4.4	8.0	12.3	2.6	4.1	7.7
Graduate degree(s)	10.6	3.8	3.7	6.5	1.5	4.0	8.2	0.0	20.5	7.2
All Groups[a]	100.1	99.9	99.9	100.0	100.0	100.0	100.0	99.9	100.0	100.1

Source: Data from 1,001 questionnaire respondents divided among the churches in the order named: 170, 78, 82, 62, 68, 100, 292, 76, 73.

[a] Details do not always add to 100% because of rounding.

Of further interest are the facts that in these nine churches, Presbyterians tended to be more churchlike than the Methodists and Baptists, respectively (see Table 10), that "downtown" churches tended to be more churchlike than those of the suburban or intermediate areas (see Table 11), that men tend to be more churchlike in their religious attitudes (see

TABLE 9

CHURCH-SECT SCORES OF ADULT GROUP PARTICIPANTS IN
NINE BAY AREA CHURCHES BY ORDER OF MEAN SCORES

Churches	N	Mean	Standard Deviation
First Presbyterian	292	75.01	11.97
Third Presbyterian	73	71.76	12.61
Third Methodist	100	71.55	11.00
First Methodist	62	69.44	12.35
First Baptist	170	65.77	13.83
Third Baptist	82	65.14	11.73
Second Presbyterian	76	64.72	11.34
Second Baptist	78	58.77	9.97
Second Methodist	68	55.96	10.73
All churches	1,001	68.36	13.40

Source: Data from 1,001 questionnaire respondents in nine Bay Area churches.

TABLE 10

CHURCH-SECT SCORES BY DENOMINATIONAL AFFILIATION

Denominational Affiliation	N	Mean	Standard Deviation
Baptists	330	63.96	12.83
Methodists	230	66.37	13.19
Presbyterians	441	72.70	12.57
Total	1,001	68.36	13.40

Source: Data from 1,001 adult group respondents in nine Bay Area churches.

TABLE 11

CHURCH-SECT SCORES BY URBAN SETTING IN NINE
BAY AREA CHURCHES

Urban Setting	N	Mean	Standard Deviation
Downtown	524	71.35	13.34
Intermediate	222	59.95	11.29
Suburban	255	69.55	12.09
Total	1,001	68.36	13.40

Source: Data from 1,001 adult group respondents in nine Bay Area churches.

TABLE 12

CHURCH-SECT SCORES BY SEX IN NINE BAY AREA CHURCHES

Sex	N	Mean	Standard Deviation
Male	267	71.08	13.81
Female	734	67.38	13.10
Total	1,001	68.36	13.40

Source: Data from 1,001 adult group respondents in nine Bay Area churches.

Table 12), and that younger adults tended to be more church-like in their characterization (see Table 13).

FIRST BAPTIST CHURCH

In many of these characterizations First Baptist Church has been something of an exception. In contrast to the various community studies and survey data this church seems to stand in opposition to the prevalent pattern. In the light of the fact that there is a good deal of current concern about the retreat of the city church to the suburbs, the obvious tendency of the religious institution to minister to a narrowly stratified segment of the social community, and the obvious failure of

TABLE 13

CHURCH-SECT SCORES BY AGE IN NINE BAY AREA CHURCHES

Age	N	Mean	Standard Deviation
18–19	15	70.47	11.00
20–24	49	68.16	13.39
25–34	192	70.63	13.48
35–44	255	70.16	13.28
45–54	171	69.02	12.96
55–64	163	65.14	12.41
65–74	123	66.05	14.34
75 and over	33	61.57	11.31
Total	1,001	68.36	13.40

Source: Data from 1,001 adult group respondents in nine Bay Area churches.

churches to successfully mix the social classes in one institution, First Baptist is a center of interest. Furthermore, the concentration upon one local church will give us a better conception of how a local church recruits a selective social base.

Chinese boxes. In considering the process by which a church builds a selective clientele for its operation it is helpful to think of various groupings as Chinese boxes that fit within each other. The largest of these boxes is a church's *universe*. It comprises all those persons for whom attendance at First Baptist is geographically possible.[18] In this case the universe comprises the metropolitan area of fifteen to twenty miles for those who utilize freeways.

The next smaller box is the *constituency* of the church. Every church has a larger number of people who consider a particular church "their church" than the number of members. Whether members or nonmembers, this is the church that they list when they are asked to state a church preference. This is the church that they come to for celebrations such as Christmas and Easter. This is the church that they approach when they need the services of a clergyman for a funeral, wedding, or personal crisis. To provide for the constituency and to utilize it as a possible evangelistic potential, a local church will usually have two mailing lists—one to the members, and the other to the members plus other interested parties.

The next smaller box is the *membership*. The membership comprises those who have assented to immersion baptism and accepted the membership vows. More is expected of members than of those not formally received into membership. A church usually does not feel apologetic about presenting the financial and other needs to these people.

On the other hand, one should not jump to the conclusion that all members demonstrate an active concern for the welfare of the church. For example, the influence of a Baptist background may lead a family to transfer its membership to First Baptist when they move into the area, only to become aware later that this church is different.

A still smaller box is the Sunday morning *congregation*. This, of course, is not the same group every Sunday morning, for only about one third of a congregation's membership is in attendance on a single Sunday. (First Baptist had a slightly better record than the average.) Within the Sunday morning congregation there is a solid core of "nuclear" members who are in attendance every Sunday, those "modal" members who make church about every third week, "marginal" members who attend infrequently, and the interested and curious non-members who are shopping around.[19]

Within each congregation there is a network of *established groups* that plan and administer the parish program as well as provide institutional expression. These include administrative bodies, Sunday school classes, women's circles, and other regularly meeting bodies. First Baptist has more than thirty such groups, meeting at regularly stated intervals, that provide a variety of interests and social situations.

The tiniest of the Chinese boxes is the small *intimate fellowships* that frequently meet in the homes of the active members. These comprise the monthly class socials, the small prayer groups, the volunteer committees, and the undesignated informal friendship cliques that frequently meet for other purposes but also relate themselves to the church.

These, then, are the social "communities" of First Baptist Church. These communities can be identified in every church, but their extensive development in First Baptist provides an opportunity for closer study and the recognition of more unique features.

Sunday morning congregation. The "front room" of the church is the sanctuary, and there is an "open house" in the front room every Sunday morning. Here is the place where the church places its best foot forward and where the church makes a bid for the attention and loyalty of the community about the church. During the week the order of worship with news of the parish is mailed to all who have indicated an interest in the church. The announcement of the Sunday morning worship services receives front-page billing. The choir has rehearsed its anthems until it can perform to perfection. The ushers have been well coached in the movement of groups and individuals in and out of the service with an air of "glad you could be here—come again." The service moves psychologically to the climax when an invitation is extended to "unite with our church and become a part of its fellowship."[20] Because past experience has indicated that most people do not "come forward" the first Sunday, a registration of attendance will indicate those who "ought to have a call."

The people who are in the sanctuary on any given Sunday are a group made up largely of the members of the church, the "friends" of the church who have not as yet joined, visitors, and those persons who are serious about church membership *if* they can find the right church. In the main, this last group is the one to which the service will be pitched by a persuasive appeal to become a part of the institution.

However, most of these people will also have had some contact with a Baptist church previously. Many Southern whites immigrating into the Bay Area will look for a large Baptist church in the area which will have an outstanding preacher, choir, and well-developed program. Many Southern Baptists coming from the rural, conservative, Bible belt of the South will be shocked with the character of the service because it does not represent their image of a Baptist church.

On the other hand, succeeding generations of First Baptist offspring have been exposed to the "secular" influence of the Bay Area, taken advantage of the rapidly expanding educational system of California, joined the expanding white-collar strata, and been influenced by the theological sophistication of such institutions as Berkeley Baptist Seminary. It is in the context of such a varied religious and sociological milieu that First Baptist Church attempts to reach the man in the pew on a Sunday morning.

But the front room of First Baptist Church (as is the front room of any church) is a screen selecting from those who attend the service the persons who will later become a part of the church. It is true that the doors are open wide and the invitation is extended to all, but those who come through the door and come forward for the invitation are a select group who must believe and feel that this is an expression of religion and social compatibility that is comfortable for them. If this is not communicated, the likelihood is that they will not return again, and since the church must find one hundred and fifty persons every year to replace those who are lost before it can even gain ground numerically, considerable effort is directed toward making them regular worshipers and moving them into the working organizations and classes of the church and church school.

As one meets and talks to the people of the parish one finds that the theological rationale of the worship service is largely unknown to the man in the pew. The man in the pew comes with a theater-type orientation and the subtle pressures of institutional survival reflect this. Thus, the service moves persuasively and calculatingly onward toward a commitment to the institution. Let us look through the eyes of the church members at First Baptist to see how this screening process takes place.

First and foremost in the eyes of the parishioner is the preacher and the sermon that he preaches. When "worship service" is mentioned there is the inevitable jump to the preacher and his sermon. This is the way one young man appraised the worship service when it was mentioned:

> The thing that I really enjoy is the preaching. The rest of the service is important too, but the preaching is what makes it. The service is a feeling of God and a support of God. One should pray to God too . . . but the message is what is most interesting. . . . The Psalms, etc., don't really do much for me.[21]

A young woman, one of the few who appraised the preacher negatively, also jumped straight to the minister in her appraisal of the worship service:

> I don't respond to Dr. —— (senior clergyman) as a pastor because I don't think that he is any more spiritually developed than I am. —— (associate minister) is different; —— (minister of Christian education) is also developing and is really coming through. Dr. —— is doing a good job of administration and

program but is interested in the dramatic. . . . I just feel that there isn't the humility there should be. . . . You asked me to talk about the worship service and I have talked about the ministers, but that is the way it affects me. . . . I have to go to other churches to get the spiritual growth that I need.[22]

Such negative response to the senior minister was infrequently found by the researcher. In fact, the researcher who began his study with a bias against the "pulling" power of the preaching function in a church came out amazed at the way this clergyman's personal charisma, especially in the pulpit, reached out and took in the seemingly passive worshiper in the pew. One woman confessed,

I feel more of a personal relationship with Dr. ——— on Sunday morning than I do when I go to the ——— Sunday School Class.[23]

Another man reported:

During a period of depression over an experience with a girl I started going to church and liked Dr. ———. I liked the feeling of his voice. It moved me. . . . Dr. ——— is really the one who got me going back to church again. I felt that he was really talking to me personally.[24]

Some of the more sophisticated members in the church would have liked to have more sermons dealing with profound topics of contemporary living and some of the persons with Southern Baptist or Church of Christ background would have cared for more "fire and brimstone," but the researcher found that the pulpit ministry was reaching the modal man in the pew in a significant way. An extremely informal manner, warm personality, and storehouse of illustrations to tug at the heartstrings of the parishioner made the pulpit an extremely effective evangelistic feature of this church.

At the same time there was little in the message of the preacher to divide the congregation into factions. Although it would be unfair to say that there was no social consciousness on the part of the clergy, the researcher listened in vain for any divisive statements from the pulpit. On the other hand, there was an abundance of abstract phrases such as "Jesus Christ is Lord," "Ye are the salt of the earth," etc., in which every person could agree and make his own interpretation. In the main, the sermons carried the burden of persuasion— persuasion to "follow Jesus by joining hands with First Church." Sermons were not used to elaborate controversial issues.

Music was another significant factor in the cultic screen that filtered out some people and accepted others at First Baptist. When the musical expression of a church is compatible with the worshipers it can unite a strange group of people into a feeling of corporate oneness, transfer a large body of people from one movement of the worship into another, and move them to action and dedication at the close of the service. Frequently it is more effective than a confession of faith, and its symbolic language often carries a message more effectively than any other medium.

On the other hand, there are all kinds and types of music in Christian churches, and it also becomes an object of differentiation among them. Some are proud of their "long hair" taste and the quality of the music associated with the church. On the other hand, those who have been reared on gospel songs and less inhibited forms of musical expression feel greatly uncomfortable with more reserved classical expressions of church music.

First Baptist Church had made some decisions about music that served as fibers in the Sunday morning filter. The selection of a hymnal had been one of these decisions. The anthems and special numbers were also a mark of differentiation.

Pressure was exerted from time to time to introduce other forms of music, but there was no yielding to these pressures by the minister of music, who said on one occasion, "If the Catholics and the Lutherans can educate their people into the acceptance of classical music for worship and still reach the lower classes then we can too." When asked if people were conscious of such differences he responded:

Oh, yes, we have quite a few people who are aware of differences—especially the students from the air base who have come here from Southern bases. . . . But I don't let down. I tell them that I'm sorry that they have not had a satisfactory musical background, but this church has come a long way in building this kind of program and we couldn't go back to the old standards any more. . . . We tell them that they will have to learn to appreciate good music and in time they do. They come to love these great hymns and many of them will tell us so later.[25]

Although the minister of music is adamant about the musical, poetical, and theological standards which he felt must be maintained (by his own admission other churches had more sophisticated musical programs), it is doubtful if he or others realized how effective the musical program is in filtering out potential members. Comments like the following frequently came from those who did not join.

In the church I was raised in, they sang more of the peppy songs. They had more life to them . . . more spirit . . . it seemed to me, more real religion. There were more songs like the Billy Graham meetings. . . . Of course, this (hymns at First Baptist) suits my husband more because he was an Episcopalian but I don't know half of them.[26]

The ordinances[27] of First Baptist Church are also a feature of the screening process. The church insists upon immersion when persons become Christians and when people transfer from other denominations where this has not been the practice. Although more and more Baptist churches have abandoned this cultic practice as a requirement for membership (Third Baptist Church in this study does not require immersion of persons who transferred from nonimmersionist churches), First Baptist has stuck with it.

At the same time it is evident that the social consequences of this practice are demanding, and every precaution is taken to make the ordinance as socially acceptable as possible.

On Sundays when baptism is a part of the service, the draped and curtained opening is drawn for an unobstructed view of the clergyman who reads the Scriptural authority for the ordinance and baptizes the candidates as they enter from obscured accesses. Upon affirmation of Jesus Christ as Savior, each candidate is carefully immersed backward (with a handkerchief placed over his nostrils by the minister to protect the uncautious candidate). In the case of women, an attendant draws the curtain just enough to obscure the immersed candidate. A musical backdrop is rendered for the ordinance by the minister of music at the organ.

The attention given the service of baptism in a twentieth-century Baptist church has a refinement and a dramatization to it that would be unrecognized by the Baptist who lived on locusts and wild honey, preached a radical message to those who would come out from Jerusalem into the wilderness to hear him, and baptized among many others the Founder of the Christian faith. A contemporary handbook for Baptist ministers accentuates on every page not only the spiritual but the social aspects of the practice of immersion.[28] The robe must be weighted so as not to balloon or float in the water. It must be clean and of proper length. To establish confidence, candidates ought to be taken into the empty baptistry, where explanations are directed to eradicate fears and embarrassing incidents. Deacons and deaconesses are to be on hand to assist in the service. Ministers must use care in giving the candidate adequate support during the immersion. Baptistries may frequently be decorated and candles lighted. These and numerous other aspects of the ordinance broadcast the social significance of this act of worship.

In spite of the careful attention and dignity of the occasion as provided by First Baptist, there is little doubt that this aspect of the cultus is a barrier to many persons, especially those who have not been brought up in an immersionist church. One prospective member of First Baptist told the author about how his mother and father fought off the ordinance for years, yet at the same time they were very active in a Baptist church. Finally, when the minister of the church insisted that they be baptized, they changed their church activities to another church. In this particular case this young man had been active in a Baptist church most of his life, but he was still not baptized.[29]

Another young woman related her account:

> Immersion wouldn't bother me now, for I have been immersed twice, but I fought it off for a long time before I was first immersed. . . . If it wasn't for the fact that I became so active in the church and so active in the gang that went to the church I probably would never have been immersed. My brother and I were active in the young people's group and I was a soloist for the choir. . . . I got sick and the pastor was so very nice. . . . When I got married shortly afterward we both got baptized together.[30]

Another point of view frequently mentioned by prospective members questioned the theological authority of the mode of baptism by immersion. For such persons, immersion is something that is viewed on the periphery of the fellowship and not central to the value that the church has for them. One thoughtful young man put it this way:

> I think that it is kinda silly to insist upon immersion for baptism. This is just another kind of literalism, it seems to me. . . . But if I decide to join the church, and that depends upon my wife who has not yet become a Christian, then we will both be baptized in the church. . . . I don't think it's important enough to make a fuss about.[31]

Baptism at First Baptist Church, as it must be in most immersionist churches, is a cultic characteristic presenting social hurdles to prospective members in modern society. The dignity which the staff at First Baptist strives so carefully to provide reflects more than an emphasis to create a spiritual experience—it also reflects the fact that this is a social experience amid sophisticated and sober surroundings and that the participant must be protected from embarrassment and supported in every way as he makes his spiritual affirmation.

The liturgical pattern of the worship service is another limiting factor in the screen that selects a congregation from the surrounding population. For Southern Baptists moving into the Bay Area the ritual of First Baptist Church is more formal and structured than what they are familiar with, and therefore somewhat strange. On the other hand, there are those in the congregation who demand a "grown-up" religion, as one of the young adults expressed it, "like the Presbyterians and the Methodists." The order of worship for a Sunday service is as follows:

PREPARATION FOR WORSHIP
    Invitation to Worship
    Organ Prelude
WE COME INTO HIS PRESENCE
    Introit—Call to Worship
    Hymn
    Invocation and Lord's Prayer
    Witness of Baptism
WE BOW BEFORE HIM
    Preparation for Prayer
    Silent Prayer—"Be Still and Know that I Am God"
    Pastoral Prayer—Choral Response
HE SPEAKS TO US
    Scripture Reading
    Hymn
    Tidings of the Church and Registration
    Offertory, Doxology, Prayer
    Anthem
    Sermon

WE DEDICATE OURSELVES
    Prayer of Dedication
    Hymn of Dedication
    Benediction and Choral Response

To be sure, the liturgically sophisticated would not think of this as a formal worship service. There is no regular use of creed, antiphonal singing, or much consciousness of the liturgical seasons. Most conspicuous by absence are regular prayers of confession and forgiveness or assurances of pardon.

But the most discriminating act of worship separating First Baptist from all other downtown churches of the major denominations is the "invitation," not listed in the above order of worship. The service moves in steady anticipation toward a mood and attitude of commitment and dedication at the close of the service. A prayer of dedication emphasizing one's personal response to God creates a smooth and natural transition into a personal appeal from the pulpit to "accept Christ as personal Savior" and to "unite with our church and become a part of the fellowship." Although the appeal varies somewhat each week, the invitation of September 21, 1958, was not unusual. The preacher appealed:

> Now is the time to accept Jesus Christ as Savior if you have not already done so. We have a bill of sale for your signature. . . . Will you make your commitment? I hope that this hymn will reach you and I pray that you will come forward to say, "Here am I; *use* me!"

At this point the organist broke into the service with the chords of the familiar hymn, "Have Thine Own Way, Lord!" as the presiding clergy made their way down from the chancel to the front of the nave where the respondents could be met with an outstretched hand and welcomed into the fellowship. Invariably the preacher would break into the hymn between the verses to move some soul who might be wavering on the edge of a decision, with a statement not unlike the one used on this day.

> Some have come forward this morning, but I am sure that there are more of you. We have talked about this in your homes. Some of you I see up there in the balcony—some on the main floor. Now is the time. It may be later than you think.

As each respondent made his way forward, a layman came to stand by him to make the necessary introductions, to obtain information to facilitate reception of members, and to answer questions. As these sponsors took over, the clergymen made their way to the exits to greet the congregation as they left the sanctuary.

At the bottom of the Sunday morning order of worship the following is printed to extend and clarify the invitation:

An Invitation

A cordial invitation is extended to all members of the congregation to unite with our church and become a part of its fellowship. If you have never accepted Christ as your personal Savior, you may come on profession of your faith in him. If your membership is in a church somewhere else, you may come by transfer of church letter. If you have lost your connection with some church to which you formerly belonged, you may come on reaffirmation of your faith. Response to this invitation may be made by coming forward during the singing of the last hymn or by speaking to the pastor at the close of the service.

Also of significance in the screen that differentiates this congregation from others in the Bay Area are the physical surroundings as well as the images conveyed by the furnishings of the sanctuary. The chancel is built into one corner of a large sanctuary and features the pulpit in the center of a raised platform. Immediately below the pulpit is the Communion table and above and behind are the choir loft and the draped baptistry. The chancel is plainly paneled with a modest amount of ornamental carvings and an array of ornamental organ pipes. A cross rests on the edge of the baptistry but is removed from the sanctuary when baptism is administered. The flowers usually present a more imposing center of attention on Sunday morning than the cross.

Perhaps the prospective church member will notice more quickly the robes of the clergy and the choir, for even such simple vestments frequently become an obstacle to the migrant Southern Baptists who are moving into the Bay Area with increasing frequency. Remarked one such church attender after his first experience with First Baptist Church, "I was shocked to see not one, but three, robed clergymen on the platform at one time." In speaking of this group of prospective members, the pastor was undoubtedly correct when he said: "We have a lot of Southern Baptists in the congregation but not all stay. I think the biggest shock they get is when they see me in a robe."[32]

These are some of the more apparent acts of cultic expression that prospective members and alienated individuals could identify as being troublesome hurdles for them as they attempted to become a part of the membership of the church. They are cited not to exhaust the list but to establish the fact. The necessity for further research at this point became apparent again and again when individuals could not put their fingers on some of the things that repelled them or attracted them, although they conscientiously endeavored to identify them. Some details of the front room of the church remain a mystery, but a front room it undoubtedly remains. First Baptist has from forty to fifty new persons in its sanctuary every Sunday morning. Some will come again to survey the worship and perhaps to take part in it. Most of them will not return. Only a small portion will eventually make their way into the "back rooms" and become a part of the fellowship.

Established groups. As one moves from the "front rooms" to the "back rooms" he becomes involved in more socialized differentiation. In the sanctuary each meeting is designed, directed, and controlled by the clergy. Personal relationships tend to be more secondary than primary, for conversation with one's neighbor in the pew is restricted and attention is directed toward the chancel. Although the screening process just described is selective, the test of social and religious compatibility becomes more acute as the individuals of the congregation are moved into the back rooms where Sunday school classes, women's circles, choirs, administrative bodies, etc., meet with regularity.

The small group is the most important type of group experience upon which the contemporary church must depend for its existence. Although it has not been recognized as such, the development of small groups has been the organizing principle around which churches have developed. As one moves into these groups he finds that the leadership is vested in the hands of the laity and primary-type relationships are more characteristic of the social situations. In these small groups where coffee and doughnuts lubricate the vocal chords even in the Sunday school classes, and where the influence of group dynamics techniques has made the circle something other than the symbol of eternity, there is abundant opportunity for social involvement. Name tags are provided for the easy identification of the stranger, and conscientious greeters in almost every group see that introductions are made and a friendly hand extended. In brief, the tendency is definitely toward more intimate social relations.

One of the aspects, so frequently overlooked by churchmen and others who have come to appreciate the strong bonds of friendship that are developed in primary relationships, is the fact that in these relationships great strains are placed on individual differences. The individual must find satisfaction with the organizational structure that inevitably develops in every group situation. Distinctions of class, status, and power now stand out in bold relief at close range. Religious attitudes and traditions now are put side by side with other attitudes and traditions, and uncomfortable distinctions are now made that just as frequently produce estranged relationships as they

provide the cement for group cohesion. As those who attended the Sunday morning service are referred to the group
leaders for cultivation, these persons are introduced to another screening process. If, after a number of sessions together
the experience is not satisfactory, attendance becomes more and
more infrequent until eventually the person is dropped from
the roll of the group.

This deletion, in turn, is reflected in the Sunday morning
attendance, for those who do not develop strong social ties
with others in the small groups become infrequent attenders
or lose interest in the church altogether. Thus there is a definite relationship between the number of small groups in a
church and the size of its congregation on Sunday morning.

It is here in the small-group structure of First Baptist
Church where we receive our most significant insight into the
"deviant" character of this church. Previously we noticed that
this church seemed to stand in opposition to stratifying characteristics of the other churches. First Baptist had approximately thirty different groups of people meeting regularly.
When fourteen of the groups with some educational objectives were surveyed for this study, it was discovered that this
church was more successful than any other in providing a
group for everyone.

This was most vividly revealed in the church-sect scores.
To begin with, First Baptist Church took the median position
in the nine churches surveyed. Its appeal seemed to be directed at the middle range of Protestants in this study. Secondly, it had the largest standard deviation of any church in
the study. This would indicate that a wide range of religious
attitudes were incorporated in the church. When considered
as a total congregation, their religious attitudes did not cluster
as closely around the mean as did the other churches. But the
break-through did not come until the groups were studied
individually. In Table 14 we can see that the means of these
fourteen small groups had a greater range than did the means
of the nine churches. (See Table 9.) In short, the stratifica-

tion continued to be characteristic of this church, but it was provided by the small groups rather than by the church as a whole. Considerable freedom for this to take place was evident, as was the freedom to shift from group to group if one did not find the right group on the first try.

TABLE 14

CHURCH-SECT SCORES OF ADULT GROUPS IN
FIRST BAPTIST CHURCH

Adult Groups	N	Mean	Standard Deviation
Roger Williams	9	72.78	10.90
Young Adults	7	77.42	11.00
Partners	18	63.39	14.86
Comrades	31	72.45	13.93
Fellowship	22	67.50	15.38
First Things First	13	58.61	9.94
Business and Professional Women (morning)	6	66.33	10.83
Business and Professional Women (evening)	12	66.50	10.78
Women's Missionary Society			
Circle 1	5	58.40	14.68
Circle 2	10	65.19	10.64
Circle 5	10	60.49	6.02
Circle 6	9	61.44	10.84
Circle 7	13	59.30	12.03
Circle 10	5	56.20	15.07
Total	170	65.77	13.83

Source: Data from 170 respondents in 14 adult groups of First Baptist Church.

Intimate fellowships. The innermost of our Chinese boxes can be identified in the groups that meet in homes for monthly socials, prayer cells, volunteer committees, and social cliques. These situations demand an even more intimate relationship and consequently give the most strain to any personal differentiation.

For example, First Baptist is attempting to incorporate its blighted neighborhood in its fellowship at the same time that it attempts to hold on to its members who live in better residential districts. In an unsophisticated way we might say that social status can be measured in feet above sea level. The people in the blighted lowlands around the church found it exceedingly difficult to be a part of the intimate groups that met in middle- and upper-middle-class homes opened to them through their church affiliation in the hills.

This was well illustrated by the family who lived in the same block as the church in the top of a garage on the back of a lot. This shipyard worker had joined the church two years previous to the researcher's interview and began meeting with a church school class at that time. He stopped attending the class and the church when it became necessary to meet in the homes of some of the members on the hill. Stated the mother of this family: "We went out a couple times to class socials, sometimes only for coffee and doughnuts, but we could not invite them back here. They say we shouldn't feel this way or be ashamed of this place, but of course we really are."[33]

One could also see this same situation take place in the involvement of the various racial groups. At first they would be seen attending the worship service on Sunday morning, perhaps making their way to the balcony where they could still enjoy some measure of psychological and geographical detachment. Then they would attempt a Sunday school class if invited and encouraged by the members. But the last step would be steady attendance at the social functions that met in the homes of the people on the hills. When this study was made, no regular attendance by anyone but Caucasians was identifiable in the homes. If and when this does come about, it will undoubtedly be a major victory for the interests of racial integration at First Baptist Church.

Through such a system of Chinese boxes the selective social

base of a church may be described. In the main it is a process of "shaking down" a population through a religio-sociological screen on a number of levels until the compatibility required by that level is satisfied. First Baptist Church was something of an exception for three reasons. First, it was drawing from a wide range of religious backgrounds even though most all of them have been labeled as Baptists. Conservative, rural, Southern Baptist migrants have been moving into the area and looking for a Baptist church while at the same time urban, upwardly mobile, "high church" American Baptist influences have exerted pressures in the other direction. Secondly, a pulpit with strong personal charismatic appeal pitched a message successfully to the modal man in such a way that any strong divisive statements allowed considerable latitude of personal interpretation. Thirdly, by avoiding considerable differentiation in the pulpit on Sunday the burden of stratification was passed on to the back rooms until there was a multitude of "little churches" within the larger whole. A multitude of internal groupings provided a range of internal stratification that is rare in churches.

SELECTIVE RECRUITMENT FOR RELIGIOUS ADULT EDUCATION

Throughout this chapter we have discussed the processes and factors in the determination of the selective social base of adult groups in the church. Let us now lift out a few of the significant observations.

First, the adult group participants come into their associations through an intricate array of sociological phenomenon which serve to provide a relatively homogeneous social base for the educational process. These participants bring a certain external set of sentiments, activities, and patterns of interaction.[34] This, of course, builds a social solidarity for institutional cohesion but raises some interesting questions about the character of adult education in such a setting. Are the individual frames of reference broad enough to give adequate consideration to vital issues? What limitations are observable in the selection of educational topics? What differences in methodology are observable between the extremes of church and sect? What differences are observable in terms of resources utilized? How do solutions to social problems in different religious institutions vary? To what extent can liberal education be realized? Although some very tentative observations were naturally made in the course of this study, the limitations of this study made thoroughgoing explorations impossible. Obviously, the numerous social settings for adult education need much research in the light of their own peculiar selectivity.

Secondly, institutional affiliation dominates adult education in the church. As we have seen, the peculiarities of the "front room" largely determine the affiliation of the church members. In the majority of instances the experiences in the sanctuary must be satisfactory or there will be no participation in the small groups. This experience usually comes first in time sequence. Although there were a few exceptions to this trend in the nine churches of this study, the great bulk of adult group participants had been a part of the stream of people who flowed through the open doors on Sunday morning and then into the classrooms and small groups of the church.

Thirdly, the institution has a very tenuous hold upon the participants in its adult groups. Throughout this sociological web an "other-directed" institution has been described in which the religious clientele are in a "buyer's market" with an array of religious experiences to select from and a freedom to transfer affiliation at will. This places tremendous strain upon an institution that may be characterized as an old-line institution with built-in rigidities to accent conservatism and mediate against sudden accommodation to the fast pace of changing society. A degree of accommodation is possible, but when it becomes easier to change religious affiliation than accommodate to strange sentiments or activities then a shift can more easily be made. Therefore, in so far as tradition allows it, the church will necessarily adopt a catering relationship with its clientele because of the desire for their affiliation.[35] Churchmen must weigh the activities of group life against the possible alienation of church members and/or the winning of new members.

Such a dilemma naturally tempers the experiences within the adult groups of the church. There is understandably a reluctance to bear down upon unpopular topics, interpretations, and solutions for problems when there is a danger of alienating institutional support. In a very real sense the institution is held captive by its clientele and the freedom of the educational leadership is limited.

Lastly, the tendency toward informal organization and the primary relations in the small groups accents the process of differentiation in more intimate personal relations and serves to stratify more narrowly the adult group participants. Much of the emphasis upon primary groups has served to accent the strong bonds of intimate friendship of the members in these small groups. Little has been said about those who failed to identify with the group or drifted away when differentiations have been accented. The observations of this research would urge a second look at the theoretical orientations of Robert Bales,[36] E. D. Chappel,[37] W. F. White,[38] George Homans,[39] Arensberg,[40] and others that stress the basic concepts of action, interaction, and situation. It would likewise urge that more attention be given to those persons who have been members of small groups but have discontinued their affiliation. Not all of the insight about small groups can be gained from the people that remain.

Thus small adult groups in the church tend to be narrowly stratified, constantly changing, informal associations of church members, in which controversial issues tend to be avoided, the religious institution supported, and primary relations accented.

Chapter IV

THE ROLE OF THE
BUREAUCRATIC STRUCTURE

THE GROWTH of large-scale organizational structures in modern society is one of the commonplace developments that even the casual observer of contemporary society does not miss. The idealization of the individual as an autonomous, active integral of society, moving about independently and making his influence count where he wills, has been dealt a mortal blow. Today individual action is channeled through organizational structures in the exercise of influence. Through what has been called by some the "organizational revolution" and by others the "nucleation process," power is being expressed through a pyramiding of organizational structures. A pluralistic society of large-scale organizations has taken shape that often leaves the individual a lone voice "crying in the wilderness."

It is through such institutional power centers that styles of life are being created, obsolescence is built into production, new wants are formed and abolished, values are being shaped, and standards formed. Real values and character-building influences are not formed as often by school, church, or home, but by some advertising agency, Hollywood studio, publishing syndicate, labor union, or trade association. Culture is big business in America, and everyone wants to be big enough to make his influence felt—doctors, poultrymen, teamsters, engineers, veterans.

It is in this fashion that power, centralizing in one institutional sphere, has called forth its "countervailing powers" in other areas. It is not surprising that as "big business," "big farmer," "big government," and "big labor" began to exert more and more influence upon the American scene, pressures toward "big church" would also exert themselves. As the church became shunted off more and more to a marginal position in a side eddy of the main stream of American life, it is not surprising that tendencies toward large-scale organizations emerged in order that the church might compete, and the bureaucratization of the institutional structures spread to make the work of the church more efficient.

Let us now see where adult education lies and how its existence is significantly conditioned by the large-scale structures of the church.

INTERDENOMINATIONAL STRUCTURES

Although interdenominational religious organizations are not large-scale in the sense that they have large budgets and a proliferation of staff officers and other paid personnel (the National Council is something of an exception), they are large-scale in the sense that they co-opt leadership, frequently from a high level, and co-ordinate a broad range of interests through other denominational structures for the total religious enterprise. It is for these reasons that they are included here.

When interdenominational activities were explored on the local level in this research, responses had considerable range, but in general both laymen and clergymen indicated an indifferent or extremely weak identification with these organizations. It often appeared that these organizations had symbolic rather than functional purpose for their affiliates. Many laymen had no knowledge whatever of the activities of interdenominational bodies. Secondly, there is a multiplicity of such bodies in the Bay Area that fragment the work of the metropolitan area into undeveloped and relatively un-co-ordinated structures. Although some other large metropolitan areas have developed extensive organizational structures, the Bay Area has never successfully united the numerous councils and associations, and this does not appear to be a near reality. In the absence of any interdenominational organization for the Bay Area, small councils and small ministerial associations perpetuate the fragmentation, although the Northern California–Nevada Council of Churches attempts to service the area with its annual budget of $60,000 spread through eight departments and twenty-nine different commissions.

Since small councils and ministerial associations with the aid of state councils characterize most of the interdenominational expression of religion in our country, attention is here focused upon them. To get at the heart of the matter two further characteristics have been selected for emphasis.

Peripheral program development.   Every council carefully avoids duplicating the work of local churches or denominational headquarters. The work of the interdenominational organization must supplement already existing denominational work rather than compete with or take over existing functions. The Oakland Council of Churches makes this emphatic in one of its current brochures:

> The Council cautiously avoids duplicating the effective efforts of denominational specialists. Our Council program is Complementary, *not* Competitive. We seek to supplement, and coordinate, all services comprehended within the orbit of our various departments. We seek to stimulate a "togetherness" that is not simply a cozy term or an emotional cliché—but a sound, practical, vital reality in service.[1]

In an interview with a council officer the same thesis was reiterated:

> If we just carry on what churches are already doing, these programs become controversial. We have to pick up a *real need* that is not being met and do something about it. . . . Of course

some of the traditional programs like ecumenical worship can still be carried out but this alone will not build a council budget.[2]

One of the constant objectives of a council is to pick up a type of service that is legitimate and *central* to the work of the church without encroaching upon the already established activities of local churches and denominational bodies. If a council function can be seen as central to the work of the church, it has a much better chance of "building council budget." Most of the time, the council staff is doing a "selling" job about present functions that churchmen consider supplementary and peripheral. Complained another interdenominational officer: "The good that we have been doing is unknown. We need better ways of communicating what is being done."[3]

The type of thing that interdenominational organizations like to pick up and take over is illustrated in the March 1959 issue of *The Church at Work:*

> The Council's current venture into television, "Man and His Problems," with Alexander Miller, is approaching—by industry standards—the fulfillment of a producer's dream: The show is being watched and talked about! . . .
>
> Letters tell us of some 200 little clusters of people who gather at 9:30 Sunday mornings to follow the telecast. The "Pulse" rating indicates a total audience of 20,000 viewers per program —good for the Sunday cartoon ghetto. . . .
>
> The Department of Radio–TV for the Council senses that it has discovered a use of television that may warrant sharply defining its activity to this utilization of the medium. The National Council of Churches can create dramatic programs with large budgets: we here have no such resources. Possibly, with our wealth of fine Christian professors, our contribution should be in the area of adult religious education via the 21-inch screen.[4]

But many functions that the interdenominational organization may attempt to take over and co-ordinate in a more efficient manner meet with frustration. For example, the Bay Area has no well-co-ordinated plan for church extension. Each denomination must set up its own machinery for this purpose. Some of the larger denominations have a full-time staff to give leadership and concerted action to the establishment of new churches. Others may merely have committees that are heavily loaded with other responsibilities charged with this additional objective. True, new church sites are cleared through the Department of Comity of the State Council, but there is little doubt that a more efficient plan for all denominations involved could be provided through an interdenominational center for church extension and field survey. But, as Michels has pointed out, organizations frequently become ends rather than a means to an end.[5] Step by step, high objectives are surrendered or less efficient means are utilized to gain objectives in the interest of increased organizational (denominational) strength.

Another indication that the work of the councils is complementary rather than competitive is revealed in the conflict of dates that invariably enter into the planning of council program. When so many different denominations and/or local churches are involved, conflicts in the schedules are unavoidable even with the most careful long-range planning. When these conflicts appear, it is clear that it is not the interdenominational agency that claims the loyalty but the denominational and local church programs. The rule seems to speak for itself: after the denominational and local church programs —*then* the interdenominational work.

Support from the elite. A second major acknowledgment that propels one far in such a brief commentary on interdenominational organizations is the observation that interdenominational bodies do not gain their support from a broad base of lay participants but from the religious elite among the clergy and laity. With few exceptions, such as the radio and television ministries, institutional chaplaincies, occasional ecumenical worship services, and a few modest welfare activities, the services of interdenominational organizations do not directly build a clientele among the masses of the people. Most of the services are to local churches and denominations and reach the rank and file indirectly. Even the "grass roots" conferences are grass roots only in the sense that they reach the clergy and the already active laity in the local churches. Because of this the interdenominational bodies have never developed any independent authority through large memberships that could be used as leverage to gain organizational advantage with the denominational bodies. Instead a pattern can be seen in two vital areas of organizational existence, i.e., finance and leadership.

Prior to 1958 the Oakland Council of Churches was in serious financial trouble. The Council has been operating "in the red" for a long period of time. During 1957 the matter of finances became a major crisis in the organization. The report of the Chairman of the Committee on Business Affairs and Finance in the Annual Report indicates the direction in which a council goes and the response that comes when such an organization is forced to the wall.

> Although the writer's tenure as Chairman of the Committee on Business Affairs and Finance dates only from September, 1957, a word or two of background covering the period prior to September would be in order at the outset. The Oakland Council of Churches has passed through its "times of trouble" financially, during 1957. The Executive Director left at the very beginning of the year, with considerable back salary due him, and it became necessary early in the year to reduce the size of the paid staff. It is not the purpose of this report to attempt to answer the question of why the Council was in such financial extremity. The simple fact is that there was not enough money to continue the previous year.
>
> During the spring and the early summer months, especially under the leadership of the President, Walter A. Mueller, and our new President, William P. Mott, Jr., a financial "crash" program was conducted in order to keep the Council solvent at all, and to begin to rebuild for a stronger future. This emer-

gency financing proved effective in saving the Council from total disintegration. Most of the churches stood by their financial commitments for the year. Many new individuals were added to the list of interested supporters. By September, it became evident that the Protestant Churches as a whole, and scores of individuals in Oakland, were demonstrating that the Council must continue and enlarge its program as a vital force in the community. . . . Contact was made through the members of this committee, with the constituent churches of the Council. They were asked to make their commitments for the year 1958. Results of this effort are shown by the fact that almost $14,000 has been pledged by member churches toward the basic budget, as well as definite commitments toward specific programs. These results gave great encouragement to the Executive Committee of the Board of Directors in its planning for the 1958 program. . . .

The financial undertaking of the Committee in 1958 was the elimination of the remainder of the deficit under which the Council had been for so long operating. An appeal brought in some $865, and, in addition to the regular receipts from the churches and other sources of revenue, made possible the wiping out of the deficit, and the beginning of 1958 with a small balance.[6]

These two sources, (1) the local churches that provide for council work in their annual budgets and (2) the nuclear lay members of these churches, are the major sources of support for a local council of churches.[7] A survey of the listing of individual contributors, which is included in the annual reports of the councils, reveals that almost without exception the individuals are those upon whom the local churches and denominations also depend.

On the state level a significant adjustment must be made in the sources of receipts for council operations. Again the support is from the churches, but in these bodies the support shifts from the local level to the denominational bodies on a higher level.[8] The same is true for the National Council.

Thus, financially the council must get in on the budget of

the denominational agencies and/or the local churches if it is going to undergird any program of its own. A significant secondary source is through active lay people in these churches. Since both major sources of financial support for interdenominational activities draw from the resources that local and denominational bodies could easily spend on their own program, the resistances to interdenominational activities are considerable and the budgets are difficult to increase.

Furthermore, the leadership problem also accentuates the resistances to the development of interdenominational agencies. Since the church councils do not have services that bring the rank and file into frequent contact with the councils, they are also dependent upon the churches for their leadership. It is understandable, then, that councils co-opt religious leadership and draw upon their prestige and services. When annual meetings are planned for councils of churches, the most distinguished religious leaders of the community and the nation speak for the cause of co-operative Christianity. When departments and commissions are set up to do the work of the council, the same phenomenon takes place.

This, as might be expected, raises some problems. If the job is to deliver an address, render an invocation, or pronounce a benediction, the problems are minor. But when the church leader or the denominational official is charged with the responsibility of his own institution and pressed at many points for leadership and service in this arena, interdenominational activities are frequently slighted. Providing leadership through co-optative means leaves much to be desired, as the Chairman of the Commission of Adult Work in the Northern California–Nevada Council of Churches explained:

> Prior to 1950 the adult work was going well with a program of leadership education and inspiration. In 1950 it was decided that more should be done but nothing developed before I was asked to head up the work in 1957. . . . Denominations had been asked to provide the committee but when I followed up the names some of them didn't even know that they were on

the committee. . . . In this work everything goes along fine until the denominational leadership loses interest and then things drop. Most denominational state leaders are so filled up with other denominational duties that they have no time for this work. This is what happened in the Adult Commission. Now we are working on setting up the organization on an entirely different basis. We are trying to find people who are really interested and then have them O.K.'d by the State Council and denominations. . . . Our hope is to get people who are really interested in adult work in their various localities and build an organization and program that will come out of local needs.[9]

It is quite understandable that "denominational state leaders are so filled up with other denominational duties that they have no time for this work." The careers of clergymen are not functionally related to the interdenominational phases of the ministry. They must answer to local congregations and denominational officials. If laymen are drawn out of the church to participate in interdenominational work, it also means that there will be fewer leaders to promote the program of the local church or the denomination.

Laymen's School of Religion. If one of the objectives of a council is to pick up a type of service that is legitimate and central to the work of the church without encroaching upon the already established activities of local churches and denominational agencies, then it would not be surprising that encroachments upon this objective would be enviously looked upon by the councils. This became a reality in April, 1959, when some thirty interested persons—seminary officials and professors, denominational officials, ministers, directors of Christian education, and laymen—made plans for what has since become known as the Laymen's School of Religion. When the school opened in Berkeley in the fall of 1959, two hundred and fifty students enrolled from eleven denominations, and sixty-seven churches, and thirty-three communities of the San Francisco Bay Area.[10] Edward S. Setchko, writing in *The Christian Century,* described it as follows:

Here is a long-term endeavor to offer a systematic opportunity for laymen to delve deeply into all areas of theological thought as they are related to man's search for meaning and purpose in this world. The school came into existence because of the hunger on the part of a great many people for the chance to be involved in the kind of corporate search which would enable them to share more adequately in the total ministry of the church.[11]

Without a doubt the denominational and interdenominational bodies had failed to read the "signs of the times" and had been "scooped" in their own business. By the spring of 1960 five hundred students (eleven students had come from the nine churches of this study) enrolled in the Laymen's School of Religion, and it was expanding its campuses to a wide range of locations throughout the Bay Area. By the time that the denominational bodies decided that they would be willing to provide support and councils of churches were willing to develop organizational units within their structures to encompass the new school, the administration and faculty of the school had decided that they would risk financial instability for freedom and autonomy. The embarrassing part of the whole affair for the councils was that it was so interdenominational and truly ecumenical in spirit!

Not incidental to our study is the manner in which the Laymen's School was started. Rev. Muriel James, ordained minister and first dean of the school, can be given the major credit for the school's existence. Mrs. James brought to the school considerable civic experience in adult education, contacts from course work in a number of seminaries, an unusual ability for hard work, experience with the frustrations of "institutionalism" from staff experiences as a minister of Christian education in local churches, and a dedicated charismatic personality that readily spreads her spirit of personal enthusiasm. Another important factor in the inauguration of the school was the fact that Mrs. James was engaged in graduate work in adult education at the University of California at Berkeley in the pursuit of a doctorate.

Although this particular adult education endeavor is something of an exception to the usual pattern of adult education with which this study has been primarily concerned, it can be numbered among several centers[12] throughout the country that have attempted to supplement the low-pressure church school educational programs with a more demanding theological diet.[13] It also bears watching because of its resistance to traditional institutional structures of denominations and councils of churches. Mrs. James has stated, "The school should be free but responsive to make its contribution to the reformation of the church."[14]

Time will have to tell how free and responsive the Laymen's School can remain. As of this writing, the sponsorship of the seminary faculties and administration appears to give this toddling stepchild support, and since the seminaries have had years of experience in building their own financial foundations with limited support from denominational treasuries, the school has knowledgeable consultants. On the other hand, Mrs. James admits that her forte is not in building budget and has entertained the possibility of an administrative assistant. At the time of this writing the financial picture seemed precarious, but the school was in the process of building a social base through its own clientele, good publicity, strong co-opted leadership from the seminaries, and selected leadership from the community at large. In addition the faculty had faced the financial bottleneck and decided that if necessary it would teach without salary. Explained Mrs. James:

> We may have to do some tentmaking in order to continue. It was a real experience to see the faculty come to the decision of teaching without remuneration, if necessary. . . . Right now we are not certain that money is necessary anyway.[15]

Whatever else may be said, this new venture toward an informed laity has had an encouraging response of interest and affiliation which did not come through the efforts of the councils of churches or the denominations, but through the vision and efforts of one individual with professional experience and training, a contagious personal charisma, and the personal resources and willingness to invest considerable energy in a pilot project. How the next generation of leadership will serve this "long-term endeavor" in adult education to solve its problems and satisfy its needs will have to be seen. However, it will not surprise the social scientist if considerable organizational structure emerges and the Laymen's School reflects the institutional character of the seminaries (or other denominational or interdenominational bodies if their sponsorship is deemed necessary) upon whom they are dependent. Furthermore, it would not be surprising if administrative leadership emerges with distinctive abilities of building institutional security.

Adult education and interdenominational bodies. On the basis of the above observations, the following generalizations may now be put forth concerning adult education under the sponsorship of interdenominational bodies.

1. *Since interdenominational agencies are dependent upon denominational structures for leadership and support, adult education under their sponsorship is subject to the marginality that characterizes the denominations.* Interdenominational agencies are large-scale organizations in the sense that they are connecting units in the massive religious enterprise in America. Because they draw their support from the denominations instead of having access to an independent base from which to speak authoritatively, adult education under interdenominational sponsorship must reflect the marginal quality of the religious institution as a whole.

2. *When interdenominational bodies sponsor adult education it is usually considered peripheral rather than central to the work of the church.* This is the characteristic attitude of most churchmen to the work of interdenominational organizations. When an interdenominational body competes with the functions that are already carried on by other religious institutions, something of an exception occurs; but then

these programs meet significant resistances. Therefore interdenominational bodies usually take the alternative of sponsoring supplementary services and living with their added marginality.

3. *The future development of adult education under the sponsorship of interdenominational bodies will continue much the same as in the past except for the possibility of picking up new services.* These services, like the television program that was cited, meet an organizational need of the church, and are activities not already provided by denominational bodies. In brief, interdenominational bodies will have to be on their toes to develop new avenues of adult education before denominations get in the act if adult education is going to develop significantly under interdenominational sponsorship.

4. *Adult education under the sponsorship of interdenominational bodies will continue to be hampered by the fragmentation resulting from numerous, un-co-ordinated small units, which drastically limit the resources available to develop new programs.* Serious limitations are now evident by the lack of a full-time staff member in any state or local council charged with the sole responsibility of adult education. It is also evident in the lack of resources available even to state councils to move into the mass media in a more significant fashion. Liberal grants from individuals and foundations would help considerably to get new programs off the ground and "sell" them to denominational sponsors.

5. *That councils of churches have no corner on adult education on an interdenominational scope has been demonstrated by the Laymen's School of Religion.* This also suggests that if councils of churches do not provide educational opportunities for adults, others may be prompted to do so. The seminaries in this instance are another type of institution that has demonstrated a willingness to sponsor programs of adult education for the laity.

6. Although the number of observations is limited, the *lack*

*of professionally trained educators in the ranks of the coun-
cils limits the role of the church in adult education.* The
councils have not added staff with sufficient training and
resources to develop programs of adult education. On the
other hand, the presence of professionally trained educators,
as in the case of Mrs. James, facilitates the development of
program through the councils or some other medium.

DENOMINATIONAL STRUCTURES

That denominational structures can be described as large-
scale organizations goes almost without saying. Although the
three denominations in this study vary considerably in size,[16]
even the smallest demands appreciable administrative organization. The trends in our urban, industrial society toward
the development of large-scale bureaucratic structures and
the ascendancy of those who manage the process of production
and administration are not without parallel in the religious
institution. Since educational departments in these denominational bodies provide leadership, services, and material for
the educational programs in the local church and impinge
upon that program from other areas, it behooves us to appraise
their significance.

Rationale of denominational polity. Three main types of
church government characterize religious institutions: the
episcopal, the presbyterian, and the congregational. In this
study, The Methodist Church embodies a modification of the
episcopal type, The United Presbyterian Church in the
U.S.A. embodies the presbyterian type, and the churches of
the American Baptist Convention, the congregational type
of government. These types have frequently been likened to
the political types of monarchy, aristocracy, and democracy.

The episcopal organization of Methodism[17] stems from
John Wesley, founder of Methodism, who was in the episcopal
tradition of the Anglican communion. Although the years
have modified the Methodist organization, the Methodist
superintendency and the fundamentals of Methodist organ-

ization stem directly and historically from John Wesley. Today the Methodist organization represents a complicated, hierarchical form of government with the largest number of organizational divisions and subdivisions of any Protestant church body. One Methodist bishop described it as follows:

> The Methodist Church, as an ecclesiastical body, is superbly organized. The years have proved it. We commonly speak of our "connectionalism." By that word we mean that the parts are tied together, connected, related to one another and to the whole, organized for action. From the General Conference, the Council of Bishops, and the General Boards and Agencies the program of the church fans out through Jurisdictional, Annual Conference, and District organizations to the great body of our membership. Bishops, district superintendents, pastors, and laymen effectively serve, each in his own place, the ongoing program. The words of a popular hymn are especially applicable to The Methodist Church:
> Like a mighty army
> Moves the church of God.[18]

To connect this "mighty army" is a series of governmental bodies designated "conferences," tied together at the top level with the General Conference meeting every four years and composed of an equal number of lay and clerical representatives. Its actions are embodied in *The Discipline,* which is the code of law for Methodism. Juxtaposed between the General Conference and the annual conferences is a relatively weak organizational unit known as the Jurisdictional Conference that has as its main function the election of bishops. The Annual Conference generally comprises the geographical boundaries of a state and it is to this body that most of the policies of the General Conference are taken for expedition. A bishop presides over this conference and is assisted in its administration by district superintendents. At least once a year, although in the past it has been more frequent, the district superintendent presides over the Official Board of the local church, which is then designated the Quarterly Conference and given more power. Although other organizational divisions have been introduced and will be discussed below, these are the traditional bodies of the "connectional" system of Methodism.

A further distinctive feature in the rationale of The Methodist Church concerns the relationship of clergy and laity. Under this polity in the contemporary church the screening of ministerial candidates, their ordination, and their stationing in churches is solely under the direct control of the clergy.

The rationale for congregationalism as found within the Baptist[19] bodies characterized a position at the other end of the continuum from Methodism. In contrast to the Methodists, the Baptists see no justification, on the basis of New Testament evidence, for a marked distinction of privilege and status between clergy and laity. To them the distinction is merely one of "function and service." The Baptist position is well worded by Robert G. Torbet, an eminent Baptist historian:

> It has been said facetiously, yet with much truth, that the Protestant Reformation did not so much unfrock the clergy as it ordained the laity. What the quipster meant was that the Reformers did not confine the true church to those who had entered Holy Orders, but taught that it embraced every person who had committed himself to devoted discipleship in the name of Jesus Christ. This view, quite naturally, was a reaction against an institutionalized type of Christianity which maintained rigid lines of demarcation between priest and people, between Holy Orders and general communicants, between the truly spiritual believers and the carnal believers.[20]

A further distinctive feature of congregational rationale is that maximal power is placed in the local group both in the choice of the minister and the control of organizational affairs. Theoretically this polity is the reverse of episcopal polity. Furthermore, each organizational unit at the association (a group of local churches), state (a group of associations within a state), and national levels is likewise theoretically autonomous in the management and control of its organizational affairs. Besides refusing to admit any gradation in the ministerial office, it also opposes the idea of gradation in church courts. It insists that the highest judicatory is the congregation itself.

The Presbyterian Church occupies an intermediate position between the episcopal and congregational forms.[21] This form of church government is frequently compared with that of the United States Government, in which the concept of representative democracy is stressed. (However, it is noteworthy that none of the denominational systems has tolerated for long a two-party system.) The three distinguishing characteristics of Presbyterian church government are usually listed and given an apologetic as in this statement by J. Aspinwall Hodge, who states:

> . . . The three great principles of Presbyterianism—viz., government by elders, the parity of the ministry, and courts of appeals—have always been recognized in the Church of God. . . . The most ancient churches still extant, or of whose government we have information, were Presbyterian. . . . Calvin and the other Reformers derived their principles of polity and discipline from the Scriptures, and from these ancient churches.[22]

In the Presbyterian Church the ruling elders and deacons, as well as the ministers, are set apart solemnly in ordination. However, there is only one order of officials who are authorized to preach and celebrate the sacraments, namely, the ministers. The ruling elders are associated with the minister in the oversight of the people. The deacons take care of some of the temporal administration of the local church. The ministers, however, are ordained by the presbytery while the laity are ordained by the local minister.

Four judicatories are recognized in the Presbyterian Church. The session of the local church is composed of the ministers and ruling elders. The minister acts as moderator of the session and can not be deprived of this role as presiding officer without the consent of the presbytery. The next higher court is the presbytery, and it is comprised of all the ministers and a selection of elders from the congregations within the given area. This group has general oversight of the churches within its bounds as well as the ordaining of its ministers. The next higher court in Presbyterianism is called the synod. The synod is an organization comprising ministers and elders from a group of presbyteries. It is an intermediate agency between the presbytery and the General Assembly. The General Assembly, which is the highest court in the church, meets once a year to enact the laws of The United Presbyterian Church in the U.S.A. Presbyterians emphasize that this system provides for government by groups rather than by individuals in an ecclesiastical hierarchy.

The descriptions of the three organizational types of church polity that have been discussed briefly have emphasized the usual characteristics of such descriptions. Although a number of basic facts hold true, these traditional descriptions are not adequate for our purposes. We shall now look at these denominational types from a functional point of view and see that depending upon these descriptions alone is somewhat naïve.

Functions of denominational systems. When one examines the way organizational systems function, the theological rationale becomes tempered by both internal and external forces. The religious institution is no exception. A recent study of Methodism in Northern California and Nevada gave support to this fact in the religious organization. States the author:

It is important to note that throughout this study the discussion of internal adjustments is related to environmental influences. The financial demands of church life in a dynamic social situation call into being the critical debate over the increasing headquarters staff; this in turn relates to the problem of recruiting and holding church members in a multigroup society;

the "called" ministry faces the persistent issue of professionalism and the pressures of institutionalization; and factional differentiation reflects the varying kinds and degrees of institutional dilemma that is especially characteristic of a religious institution: responsible leadership must maintain the integrity of the church; at the same time, it must make such accommodations to the prevailing culture as to perpetuate the institution and keep it viable. *The result is that the administrative demands of the church as a social institution tend to take precedence over the sacred purposes and procedures.* This does not have to be so, but there are indications that it is so, nonetheless. There is a tendency for the religious institution in modern society to overstress organizational dynamics in order to maintain itself and thus be able to perform its function.[23]

There is little doubt that the religious institution has been affected by the major drifts in modern society toward the ascendancy of those who manage production and administration, the development of bureaucratic character to provide for managerial efficiency, the tendency toward concentration of power in the hands of the few, the massification of human society, the popular pressures from these masses, and the pluralistic interests of intermediary groups. It is the thesis here that these factors have altered radically the traditional characteristics of the church polity. Many of the old characteristics no longer hold for the religious institution. This can be seen in the development of the characteristics discussed below.

1. *There is a strong tendency in each denomination for the clergyman to owe his job to the denominational officers.* The functions that need to be focused upon here are those of placement and screening of candidates. There is no point in laboring this in the case of the Methodists and the Presbyterians, because these functions have traditionally been provided on the conference and presbytery levels through committees on ministerial relations. The Baptists, on the other hand, have not had this as a part of their tradition. Traditionally the local church has been able to select and ordain whom it pleased

and, in fact, still may do so. However, standardized procedures are widely recognized and accepted and reveal that tradition has been significantly altered in practice. Today *A Manual on Ordination, Licensing, and Ministerial Listing*[24] exists which describes standards and procedures remarkably similar to those of other communions. A church that is desiring ordination for one of its members arranges for him to meet with the state, associational, or permanent council for "interview and counsel," bringing to this "examining council" a written document attesting to his Christian beliefs, his knowledge and beliefs concerning Baptist history, polity, and principles, . . . and "acceptable testimony from the local church" as to his moral character, integrity, and Christian experience, and three years of theological training beyond college.[25] The acceptance of the standards and procedures of this manual by all but an occasional local congregation gives evidence of the fact that the function of ministerial screening has been largely taken over by the officials of the denomination, and the fact that ministers who hope to "get on" in the denomination should meet these standards.

Furthermore, denominational officials are instrumental in placing ministers in local congregations. One informant stated that the Executive Secretary of the Northern California Baptist Convention rarely attends a meeting but that a clergyman (often several) talks to him about openings in his area.[26] Many of the conferences he has with ministers at his office concern future employment. Another denominational spokesman stated that the officials of the American Baptist Union of the San Francisco Bay Cities assist churches in finding pastors and interim pastors, and also meet with committees of local churches to help them with employment problems.[27] In fairness let us acknowledge that these officials have the practice of suggesting more than one name to a particular church. Nevertheless, a dependency pattern is established and operates in such a way that due consideration must be given the denominational officials and their programs.

2. *There is substantial evidence to support the proposition that the dismissal of a minister is largely in the hands of the laity in the local church.* In this instance there is no point in laboring the case with the Baptist or Presbyterian groups, for it is the Methodists who represent the polity with a different tradition. The Methodist episcopacy has been the traditional storm center of the whole Methodist organization and the hub of the whole "episcopal controversy," which still exists, and concerns the right of the Methodist bishop to appoint men to their particular places of labor. Through the years the powers of the episcopacy have lost ground repeatedly. The story is an involved one and cannot be adequately told here, but it can be acknowledged that the lay power of dismissal is a part of a larger depreciation of the episcopal power in general.[28]

It cannot be denied that the final authority rests with the bishop and that when an issue is contested it is he who has to make the ultimate decision. However, some interesting developments have taken place in the relationship of the local church to its bishop. In the first place it is literally impossible for a bishop to know all his churches and the clergy under his jurisdiction. The delegation of responsibilities is unavoidable. Therefore, the bishop is no longer the key figure and the actual functionaries are the district superintendents. Yet even the district superintendent no longer has the kind of intimate contacts with the local parish or the minister that is necessary, but in his case there is no intermediate functionary to whom he may pass on these responsibilities. What has emerged, however, is a "pastoral relations committee" formed from the laymen of the local church. Among other things this committee is charged with appraising the relationship of the pastor with the congregation. Any member of a Methodist local church has direct access to this committee, and the committee has direct access to the superintendent. Although the formal powers of this committee are merely advisory, there is no doubt that the informal powers go beyond this. In reality a three-party system (client, manager, worker) has emerged and the manager (superintendent) knows well that if his clients (parishioners) are largely dissatisfied, the work of the enterprise in the particular organizational unit is seriously threatened. The superintendent does not pay much attention to a small group of agitators, but any general dissatisfaction will mean a change of ministers at conference time, almost without exception. In this study, one of the ministers in a Methodist church found himself without a pulpit in the middle of the year. However, this too is something of an exception.

These comments are not meant to indicate a nullification of episcopal authority to terminate relationships of clergymen in their pastorates, but they do indicate that the initiative has been shared with the laity and the laity does speak from a position of power when they say that a certain minister is not satisfactory to the congregation, as is evidenced by the fact that the minister is usually moved at conference time.

3. *Similar organizational units, which embody parallel divisions and subdivisions and render parallel services, have emerged out of administrative needs in each denomination.* To begin, it is profitable to notice that in each of the three denominations under study there are four strong organizations on comparable levels with similar jurisdictional scope. (See Table 15.) The fact that these similar units have developed in different organizational polity is an appreciable phenomenon that reflects the dominance of common administrative concerns. It also reflects a drift to a common administrative type of organization for a religious denomination. That there are some qualifications to these comparisons is recognized, yet these four distinct steps appear to expedite functionally the bulk of the church program under each type of polity.

Furthermore, within these four most significant organizational levels each denomination divides its structure into parallel divisions and subdivisions. For example, on each level there is a division of Christian education and subdivisions to include work with children, youth, adult, leadership, and such promotional activities as missionary, stewardship, and social action. Although slight variations occur, these aspects of the work of Christian education will be provided from the top to the bottom in each of the three denominations. And when the staff specialist goes about the routine of providing his services to the local church it is difficult to tell how his relationship is altered because of his denominational affiliation.

TABLE 15

DENOMINATIONAL ORGANIZATIONS ON COMPARABLE LEVELS

Baptist	Presbyterian	Methodist
Local church (designation varies)	Local church (session)	Local church (official board)
Association	Presbytery	District
State convention	Synod	Annual Conference
National convention	General Assembly	General Conference

4. *When new organizational units emerge or organizational adjustments are effected, they are prompted by administrative necessity rather than from sacred or theoretical rationale.* Although a four-level organizational structure seems to hold fast over the years in each of the denominations, there must frequently be adjustments due to external demands put upon the religious institution. Again these adaptations are prompted by administrative necessity. For example, there are currently dysfunctions in the presbytery and synod organizations of the Presbyterian church in the Bay Area. Neither of these judicatories has boundaries that are adaptable to the metropolitan Bay Area, which includes the San Francisco, San Jose, and Redwoods Presbyteries. However, this marriage of convenience is not satisfactory either, so there is current discussion about the necessity of reorganizing the jurisdictional span of the presbyteries within the synod.

A further example is the ascendance of the American Baptist Union of the San Francisco Bay Cities. This organization originally began as a small city mission society, but it has grown through the years by taking over functions and metropolitan territory from the Northern California Baptist Convention. Today these two organizations have essentially the same services and duplicate many of the functions of each. Although this administrative unit has been prompted by the necessity of some organization to better provide for the metropolitan area, the situation is far from static. However, it must be admitted that Baptist polity and vested interest give some security to a very awkward situation in spite of discussion of "streamlining" the organizational situation.

It is also well to note that when organizational levels are established without meeting functional needs they do not develop into strong units. Such is the case of the jurisdictional conference in The Methodist Church. The jurisdiction has remained a relatively weak organization in the Methodist system in spite of heated discussions about it recently, and important matters are commonly directed to the annual conference.

5. As we have just acknowledged, there are many common characteristics in the administration of religious institutions, although the rationale varies. In general, there is a drift toward a more centralized administration and control of the religious enterprise. In each denomination there has been a development of the denominational organization beyond the local church and an increase in the number of staff specialists charged with the responsibilities of developing and supervising the program in their respective areas. This leads us to the growing conviction that *"connectionalism" is a common characteristic of all well-developed religious denominations.*

The specialists in staff positions on each level obtain their direction from administrators in the line positions. Just as the staff personnel of a local church are described in Chapter II as being in marginal positions, so the staff specialists in each of the higher organizational levels find themselves in a marginal relationship to their managerial line officers.[29] In such a system the access of staff specialists to the local church comes through the line officer, not necessarily in the overt clearance of every contact, but by keeping the program in harmony with the general philosophies and objectives. In essence there is little if any difference between the administrative dynamics that operate to accomplish the same end that the Methodists have acknowledged all along as a part of their system of bishops aided by superintendents.

But the most revealing of all connectional patterns is the raising of funds and the route of the monetary intercourse. Some system of apportionment is the life line of the connectional system in any religious establishment. This is what makes it possible for a system of local churches to be more than an agglomeration of independent units. Without some system of collecting funds from a broad base of local churches and redirecting them by managerial design throughout the system, no connectional system could operate.

But do each of these denominations have this facility? It is noteworthy that each of these denominations provides at least a "suggested" figure for a local church's "fair share" of the denominational and benevolence budget. In each denomination there are lists published that indicate those churches which have fulfilled their quotas, and usually there is special recognition of those churches which give a certain specified percentage of their receipts to benevolences. In brief, the money does come in from nearly all of the churches and gets channeled up to the appropriate managers for dispersal to the necessary agencies. Perhaps the Baptists, who are frequently described as the most "loose-jointed" denomination of them all, provide the best illustration of connectional routing of funds. Among the American Baptists the monies go straight to the very top, the offices of the National Convention, and then filter down by the direction of the managers at this level. This is even more direct than up the conference ladder to the general offices in The Methodist Church.

In short, each of these denominations has a connectional system, when the actual dynamics of the institutions are studied. It is not a product of denominational polity but a result of the bureaucratic tendencies that increasingly characterize the religious institution in general.

Adult education and denominational bodies. It should now be evident that the traditional three-type characterization of denominational organizations has serious limitations for the understanding of the organizational structure of well-developed denominations. It might truthfully be stated that in the relationship of the minister with the parishioners, the ends of the continuum as studied in these three denominations have tended to take a form like that of the presbyterian polity. But a more basic observation needs to be made. *The blurring of denominational distinctions has come about mainly through the adoption of bureaucratic characteristics common to all large-scale organizations in modern society.*

There has been an unprecedented growth of bureaucratic characteristics in large-scale organizations in modern society. The pace setters have been industry, business, and government, with its massive armed forces; but these characteristics have also spilled over into such fields as social welfare, recreation, and religion. Churchmen have come to see that the detached congregation is ill-adapted for survival in the modern world and all sorts of "connectional" relationships have been established. These came about when churchmen observed methods that would help the religious institution become more efficient.[30] However, the unanticipated consequences have still been largely unexamined and unappreciated. When one attempts to understand the contemporary setting of adult education in denominational institutions, as well as the likely trend of future developments, an understanding of these characteristics is essential.

First, there must be understanding that the religious institution has provided for a clear-cut division of labor into departments where specialists are now hired on the basis of their technical qualifications to do a specific job. This constitutes the application of the skills and special training of individuals in a rational manner. Denominational structures now provide specialists in the areas of children's work, youth work, adult work, etc.

Secondly, an organization of officers takes shape that spells out a stratified hierarchy of authority. The stratification not only provides a system of incentive, but it facilitates communication by indicating the authority of the source, and strengthens control by locating and stabilizing authority. The authority is circumscribed and confined to areas relevant to official goals and objectives. Each of these forces tends to cause the ministry to move from a calling to a professional career. (The consequences of this shift in the area of values are tremendous.) The officer with responsibility for adult education finds himself in one of several offices in a department of Christian education. He will take direction and work out his program in harmony with the general philosophies and goals of his superiors. This does not mean that adult education of the church will be necessarily narrow in scope. It may move into the areas of missions, stewardship, or social action. However, it directs its attention to these areas not so much from intrinsic motives but from the concerns of the organization as a whole by the officers in the line.

Thirdly, standardized procedures and standardized products are the inevitable trend in religious organizations. This can be seen in education by the numerous "standards of achievement" that are promoted and in the packaged programs of adult education put out by denominational publishing houses for universal consumption throughout the denominations on specific dates. A system of standardized rules directs the operation of offices, and the organization becomes adept at disseminating knowledge about the "best" methods of teaching a nursery class or understanding the "group dynamics" of an adult class.

A fourth characteristic of bureaucratic development in the

religious institution has had more difficulty, but even here there have been some significant inroads. This is the trend toward impersonality. The place where the church has been most vulnerable to the charge of impersonality is in dealing with large numbers of people. As churches become larger and denominational organizations bring large groups together from individual churches, the religious enterprise has become more like the theater-type operation and the religious leader has had to pitch his message to the "modal man" rather than dealing individually with personality differences. In large churches the "Dial-A-Prayer" services also reflect the inability of larger units to deal personally with large numbers of individuals. Impersonality also comes into the picture when responsible officials at higher denominational levels have to plan for a group of churches and a large number of participants. Apportionments, for example, are suggested for individual churches through a scheme of weighting several statistical factors about the church and "leveling" each local church with some universal formula. In the field of education curriculum materials are planned much the same for rural as well as urban churches, for large as well as small parishes. Any planning for individual differences has to be provided on the local level.

Nevertheless, it is at this point of impersonality that the whole process of bureaucratization meets its most formidable opponents. Robert Rankin has correctly discerned these resistances and has emphasized them in his concluding discussion. Four of his list of nine implications for the adjustment of a religious institution in the modern environment are as follows:

2. The religious institution confronts the dilemma of trying to maintain its function as a familial fellowship in the face of demands for organizational efficiency which arise in modern society....

3. Adjustment to administrative authority tends to be more difficult in an institution which emphasizes brotherliness in all human relationships.

8. Adjustment to differences in status and rank tends to bring greater tensions in an institution which purports to emphasize familylike relationships, and to insist that there are no value-differences between individuals.

9. The concentration of decision-making power in the hands of the administration is especially resented in an institution which purports to welcome democratic participation.[31]

It has been resistances such as these that have checked somewhat the disenchantment which has come to the religious institution with its rapid swing into the orbit of the rational pursuit of efficiency through bureaucratic procedures. Still, there is no doubt that the religious institution has made some major strides in this direction.

As for the future development of adult education under the sponsorship of the religious denomination, we must accent the fact that there is a major dependence upon the clerical professionals for the design of the program although the lay participant is a free agent who must be satisfied. If the professionals would someday decide that the primary function of the church in modern society is to provide a well-grounded program of adult education, there is no doubt that tremendous strides would be made in this direction. At the present time, however, adult education is considered a specialty function in a staff relationship to the administrators who manage the religious enterprise. Adult education gains access to its public only through adopting and aiding the general goals and objectives of the line officers, who, in turn, reflect the current needs and problems of the organization. In this role adult education under the sponsorship of the church can be expected to reflect the basic needs and problems of the organization of the religious enterprise.

Chapter V

SECURITY AND THE LOCAL CHURCH

IF LARGE-SCALE religious organizations have become more and more rationally structured to keep pace with the trend toward efficiently organized bureaucratic bodies, then what about the local church? Has it gone along with this persistent theme in modern society? If there is a place where new groups with the new elite can emerge to challenge the traditional rationale, it is the local church. If there is an organizational level in the religious enterprise where new forms of adult education can materialize, it seems that the local level would provide this. In order to find answers to questions such as these it is necessary for us to refocus attention on the local church.

However, if any of these aspirations is going to be realized through the local church, it must be prompted by pressures that impinge upon the local unit, or the local unit must become organizationally secure enough that some of its energies can be directed into new channels of service. Are there pressures in the local church that might spawn programs of adult education with a broad range of interests? Is the local unit secure enough to enter such new channels of service or must it be continually occupied with survival? In this chapter we shall seek the answers to these questions.

RECRUITMENT

Obviously one of the organizational needs of a local church is membership. The missionary zeal of the Christian church has been one of its outstanding features. In contemporary societies it maintains this zeal, although it frequently appears indifferent and accommodating in its outreach. The religious institution directs its message to people and increasingly measures its success in terms of membership.[1]

In approaching the church's recruitment obsession we should keep in mind some of the ground already covered. In Chapter II accent was given the marginal characteristics that tend to weaken the case for a purely religious institution and encourages many compensating mechanisms. In Chapter III we described a screening process at varying levels of personal intimacy and acknowledged the recruitment of a selective social base. We have also noticed certain merchandising characteristics such as the sales persuasion of the Sunday morning sermon. The clientele of the religious institution in America appears to "buy" its religion much the same way it buys other commodities. There is freedom to affiliate and freedom to disaffiliate. Below are some additional indices that reflect the pressure for members.

1. The personality of the preacher is on the auction block today, and his salary will reflect the amount of personal charisma he can deliver to his church on Sunday morning. Although personal charisma is a difficult quality to appraise, it does include physical attractiveness, pulpit manner, and the communication of the morning message with authority and penetrating feeling. In brief, pulpit committees look for a pulpit minister with as much personal charisma as the church can afford.

This, someone might observe, is not very different from the "star" system of the theater, yet it seems increasingly to be the case. It is reflected in the day-to-day conversation of the laity who identify churches with preachers and describe the local church history in terms of the preaching leadership that has been associated with the pulpit. By contrast, the staff members in a large church may be likened to the supporting members of the cast. In many churches the term "*the* minister" is reserved for the preacher whether or not other members of the staff are ordained.

2. The construction of church buildings parallels the patterns of construction of other structures designed to appeal to a mobile population. Church sites are selected on the crossroads and main arteries of transportation so that the passing traffic will become conscious of the church. Striking architectural forms have emerged to capture the attention of the public. Large amounts of money are paid for choice property even though land might be purchased much more reasonably off the main thoroughfares. Stained-glass windows, steeples, and outstanding architectural features are lighted at night, sometimes with colored neon. Such features become the "marquee" of the church, designed to capture the attention of the passing parade of humanity. Offstreet parking, for the convenience of the clientele, has become as much a consideration for the church builders as for the supermarket owners.

3. The church in America has become publicity conscious. Local churches buy space for advertisements in the local papers rather than being satisfied with the mere listing of their names and services in standard-sized print. Free publicity in the form of articles submitted to the newspapers is a common desire. Numerous tracts and brochures are provided to introduce prospective members to the church and to sell religious values and allegiance. Every local church has a news organ, and many churches have several papers that go out to the constituency and periodically "push" a host of meetings and special events.

Occasionally a church will hire a public relations analysis of itself, but most of the time it will co-opt leadership within its own membership. In one of the churches of the Bay Area a "PR" man had made a study of the pulling power of other "downtown" churches as well as his own by slipping in and out of the balconies to take his count.

4. A further indication that the religious institution is accommodating to recruitment pressures is the increasing tendency toward liberal philosophies of church membership. The prevalent attitude in the major denominations is one that accepts people as they are, rather than insisting upon conversion prior to membership. As one clergyman stated, "You don't have to convert them before they come into the church—that is what the church is for!" Conversion from this point of view is seen as a process of growth in the faith rather than an experience that takes place at a given time and place.

By no stretch of the imagination could one say that the membership vows in the nine churches of this study were restrictive. This does not mean that they could not have been restrictive if administered and interpreted in this fashion, but conversation with members of these churches revealed otherwise. Although there is some variation, the membership vows of the major denominations include a statement about the person of Jesus Christ, the authority of the Scripture, the intention to live the good life, and support for the local and denominational organization. A brief reflection reveals that the acceptance of Jesus Christ as Savior, the understanding of the authority of the Scripture, the interpretation of the "good" life, and the conception of what constitutes support of the church vary considerably. In order that such vows be restrictive, considerable interpretation is required and numerous standards established. Instead, a broad and inclusive interpretation is given to prospective members, if any at all. In brief, membership vows do not function as restrictive covenants in most Protestant churches.

Undoubtedly the most restrictive of all standards is the mode of baptism in the Baptist churches. If this significant hurdle had not been so definitely a part of the tradition of Baptist churches, it could be more easily abandoned today. Some Baptist churches, including one in this study, do not make this requirement absolute, but when a denomination abandons such a firmly established cultic practice, it provides an indication that the pressure for recruits is considerable.

5. A further indication of the demanding pressure of recruitment is the tendency toward liberal philosophies of group legitimacy.[2] Many of the groups within the church have altered their purpose to one that swings far into the area of "pure" recreation. In couples organizations, men's groups, and the monthly meetings of Sunday school classes, the real business of the program is recreation. Repeatedly churchmen are acknowledging that there have to be social and recreational programs to get people to meetings.

Liberal philosophies of adult group legitimacy are more understandable in the light of the persistent problems that adult group leaders reported in the leadership questionnaire to the nine co-operating churches. When membership and attendance problems are looked upon as the most persistent problems that adult groups face, high standards for group membership are unlikely. (See Table 16.)

6. The registration of members is another indication that the church is eager to make contact with the newcomer and

TABLE 16

PERSISTENT PROBLEMS OF ADULT GROUPS IN THE CHURCH

Type of Problem	Frequency
Membership and attendance	29
Leadership (recruitment and training)	20
Organizational purpose not clarified	8
Scheduling difficulties	8
Transportation	6
Health due to old age	5
Social frictions	5
Intellectual differences	2
Miscellaneous	4

Source: Seventy-three adult group leaders responding to a questionnaire in nine Bay Area churches.

solicit his affiliation. A guest book is frequently used, but much more effective have been the various forms of registration cards that are introduced into the worship service. This practice, which is widespread in the Bay Area, provides a time in the worship service when everyone, members and nonmembers, signs the registration card. Although these cards give opportunity for members to request some service from the church, the cards would seldom be introduced into a worship service for this reason alone. Their processing on Monday morning reveals that their major use is the obtaining of new prospects, since the remainder are discarded except for a few changes of address and incidental messages. Frequently the registration is billed as a "ritual of fellowship" or some similar entry on the order of worship so that everyone will register and the new members will not feel conspicuous.

7. Furthermore, the attention given the handling of people in the worship service is also an indication of an "other-directed" concern that everyone feel welcome. Ushers are trained in the ways of handling people gracefully and in spotting new persons. In one of the Bay Area churches the bulletins of new members were marked with a blue ribbon, and, in most of the services, persons in the pew were encouraged to greet one another before they left the sanctuary. Greeters are frequently stationed at the doors to catch people that "get by" the ministers.

It was also noticeable in the administrative bodies of the Bay Area churches that rough spots in the handling of people or in the worship service got prompt attention and thorough consideration.

In addition to what has been said above about recruitment mechanisms, it should be stated that there is still a great deal of confusion in the minds of clergymen and laymen concerning the best investment of time and the types of programs necessary to enlist members for the church. One minister feels that he should be a frequent speaker for community affairs; another feels that he must have an extensive organization of laymen calling on new people. Some large churches think that a radio ministry will "pull" members to a church and others, that community service projects make a name for a church. Of course, there are different publics to be reached and some persons are more adept at reaching particular publics, but after this has been acknowledged there still remains considerable confusion about what works best for a particular church.

Since the pressure for recruits is a powerful one for the local church, pastor-seeking committees go out looking for preachers who can solve their recruitment needs by a strong pulpit. After sizing up their local problems, he is expected to come up with administrative know-how to "put their church on the map." The ability to utilize one's personal resources in pulpit and administrative machinery to recruit a growing base of support is largely what constitutes "success" in the eyes of the rank-and-file churchman.

Value Infusion[3]

One of the characteristics of the religious institution that meets a person on every hand is the constant outpouring of value-laden pronouncements and interpretations of religious experiences. So all-pervasive is this characteristic of the church that many people accept this as the church's sole business and think no more about it.

If we are to consider the church from an institutional point of view, we should not so easily pass by this common characteristic. We might well ask how much of the energy poured into sermons, church papers, and installation services is of divine mandate and how much from organizational necessity? How many of the emotion-filled illustrations from the pulpit are to describe the power of God in individual lives and how many are to sell the church as the setting for spine-tingling, heart-warming religious experiences? How much of the ordination service is to obey divine mandate and how much of it is to build an organization of deployable personnel? How many of the "why I am for the church" statements by prominent people are used to sell and sustain interest in the religious institution? Are the current emphases of the church purely the response to the will of the Divine, or are they responses that have arisen to meet the needs of a type of organization that must exert more and more energy to secure its values and meet its needs in a society that is becoming more and more secular?

Another profitable direction for an institutional probe is to ask about the type of activities in which a religious institution might engage if more of the culture supported its values. Would it tend to divert more resources toward social welfare, the major portion of which has already been turned over to other agencies? Would there be the same concern in its educational program for a solid theological base? Would its educational program expand into areas that would not necessarily support its institutional rationale? Would its program of social action, which most frequently develops after the rest of the program is secure, develop earlier in the institution's history and enlarge in scope? In brief, why has the energy of the church not been directed into areas other than those of current concern? Could it be that its programs of high value infusion must satisfy needs and solve problems as well as respond to the divine imperatives? It would appear that there are a number of institutional insecurities with which the religious institution must deal.

Value infusion and recruitment. With its own brand of "indifferent zeal" (which is never really indifferent) a church will push affiliation and attendance from the moment the visitor steps over the threshold. One way the church does this is to ride on the coattails of the elite in almost any realm of activity from Nobel prize winning physicists to politicians. Quotes from sermons and church periodicals are often of the following type:

SHOULD I FORCE MY CHILD?

Shall I make my child go to Sunday school and to church? Yes! And with no further discussion about the matter. Are you startled? Why? How do you answer Junior when he comes to breakfast on Monday morning and announces to you that he is not going to school any more? You know. Junior goes!

Why all this timidity when in the realm of his spiritual guidance and growth? Going to wait and see what church he will decide to attend when he is old enough? Quit kidding! You didn't wait until you were old enough. You don't wait until he's old enough to decide whether he wishes to take his medicine when he is sick; neither do you wait until he is old enough to decide whether he wished to be clean or dirty. Do you? Just whom are you trying to kid?

What shall we say when Junior announces he does not like to go to Sunday school and church? That's an easy question to answer. Just be consistent. Tell him, "Junior, in our house we ALL go to church and Sunday school, and that sure includes you." Your firmness and example will furnish the bridge over which youthful rebellion may travel into a rich and satisfying experience in personal religious living. The parents of America can strike a telling blow against forces which contribute to our juvenile delinquency, if our people everywhere (mothers and fathers) will take their children to Sunday school and church regularly.

—J. Edgar Hoover[4]

Another statement typical of those uttered by clergymen came from the pastor of Third Baptist Church and reads as follows:

This last week, I had a very rare privilege—a tour through the California Medical Facilities. This is the prison hospital where the criminally insane are treated. The work there is unique and it is the only hopsital prison like it in the world, outside of Utrecht, Holland. Twenty-one hundred men are treated there. Millions of dollars of our tax money are spent to take care of these prisoners.

What is the answer? The church has the answer—to give the complete man a spiritual life—to round out the whole of life for the individual. In short, to save a man by bringing him into an encounter with Christ and relating him to God through Christ.

But getting this answer to them is up to you! There are many aspects to this wonderful work. The thrill of knowing we have a part in such a work with God speeds us to the task.[5]

Value infusion for sustaining interest. If workers could be hired as they are in industry, the church might be able to dismiss the repetitious and time-consuming work of value infusion at an earlier stage and get down to the business of exerting influence and power in new and expanding channels of activity. In the church, however, the process of value infusion is seldom laid aside. Such items as the following reflect the need and response of the church in this area.

Did you join this church because ——————— *(Minister) promised that life with Jesus Christ could be an exciting adventure?* Have you begun to wonder just what that adventure is? Have you followed a path to a certain point and seem to be at a standstill? Have the street lights and guideposts faded out for you, so that you feel you are standing alone, groping around, restless, apprehensive? If this is *you,* cross off some other church activity and come Wednesday nights with us to the Fireside Room. Get into the life stream of your church, and you too will come to know God in all His tremendous power and love. Wednesday nights *are* an exciting adventure![6]

Not unrelated to the process of holding and sustaining interest in a local church is the insulation of the individual from the conflicting ideologies that make their bids with increasing power in today's society. One will find a nuclear core of members in every local church that has adopted a "self-image" of what the religious man is like in our kind of world. The best products of the church are the totally involved. Constant exposure to the indoctrination of the religious ideology through the value-laden mechanisms common to the church will develop a conception that will serve to insulate the individual from the conflicting values of his secular world. An example of such a product of insulation is illustrated by the following experience related by a loyal church member:

> The other day one of my laborers made a remark about a woman walking down the street. I just ignored the comment, but soon he said something again. He noticed that I didn't pay no attention. He said, "You must be a happily married man." But I told him: "No, I'm a bachelor. . . . Talking about a woman like that is just not my belief." Then he wanted to know what my belief was so I told him I had Baptist belief. . . .
>
> Over a period of time these opportunities to witness pay off. The people who have worked for me for a while know how I believe.[7]

It should not go without notice that such products of the ideological and moral community make for easy communication through the institution. A broad context of "understood" meanings ensures that the spirit as well as the letter of the message is caught. Connect the ideological with an emotional identification and easy conformity and easy practice become valuable products of the value infusion.

Value infusion for deployment of personnel. Not only must the local church win recruits and sustain their interest but it must also transform and use them as loyal, committed workers in its organizational life. Since the church is dependent upon a volunteer incentive system, it must invest a tremendous amount of energy in convincing people that service ought to be given freely. Whether the rationale for this service be humanistic or emphasize some transcendental reward system, the energy expended to enhance the system and secure the workers is considerable. Table 16 reveals that the problem of recruiting and training leaders for adult groups is second only to membership and attendance problems. In Table 17

TABLE 17

LENGTH OF ADULT GROUP LEADERSHIP

Length of Leadership	Frequency
Less than 1 year	31
1 to 2 years	20
3 to 4 years	13
5 to 9 years	8
10 or more years	2
Total	74

Source: Seventy-four adult group leaders responding to a questionnaire in nine Bay Area churches.

we see that short-term leadership characterizes these roles in the church. Rapid turnover in leadership is a persistent problem. Furthermore, Table 18 reveals that the bulk of this

TABLE 18

TRAINING OF ADULT GROUP LEADERS UNDER CHURCH SPONSORSHIP

Extent of Leadership Training	Frequency
Laymen with no special leadership training	30
Laymen with some leadership training	30
Unordained "minister" or church "worker" with some professional training	5
Ordained minister	3
Minister in training	3
Layman with some ministerial training	2
Total	73

Source: Seventy-three adult group leaders responding to a questionnaire in nine Bay Area churches.

leadership has little or no leadership training under the sponsorship of the church.

Not unrelated to the problems of recruitment and maintenance of lay leadership is the fact that those in leadership positions are often overworked. Every clergyman knows what a knotty problem is the spreading of the work load. The seventy-three leaders responding to the questionnaire held seventy-five other leadership positions in their local church, eleven leadership positions in their denomination, sixteen other leadership positions in interdenominational agencies, and thirty-one other leadership positions in civic organizations. (This data also from the leadership questionnaires.)

In essence, the technical mechanics of organizational existence must be impregnated with the ideological rationale if the religious institution is to become a viable organizational entity. The everyday work of the church steadily involves a large crew of workers to provide for classes, clubs, committees, and boards. These persons must have the motivation to give constantly of their time in the servicing of the multitude of subgroups in the local church. It is good to keep in mind that although many of the meetings of these workers (including the clergy) are billed as training sessions, large amounts of motivational material are disseminated. The following two notices from church periodicals illustrate the kinds of meetings to which ministers and laymen are frequently called.

Training for Our Ministers

Two of our Ministerial Staff, Rev. _____ and Rev. _____, are off tomorrow to a two-day Church Officer Training Institute at Asilomar. Ministers, assistant ministers, and Christian education workers from churches in all parts of the country are participating in this and a series of other similar institutes being held during these spring months. Their purpose is to provide instruction so that the ministers may, in turn, guide those in lay responsibilities in our church, especially in the program of the nurture of the church. Institutes are under the sponsorship of the Board of Christian Education.[8]

Church Officer Training

Every elder, deacon, and trustee—active or inactive—is urged to set aside Sunday evenings, Oct. 4, 11, and 18, to consider the vital subject of "The Nurture of the Church." These can be three stimulating evenings with lasting results in the work of this congregation. Read the pamphlets in preparation, then come at 7:00 P.M. on October 4 prepared to share your ideas.[9]

Value infusion and financial support. Another activity of local church program that brings a flood of supporting material to the church member via the mails, pulpit, and personal contact is the annual church financial canvass. When a thorough job is done, a tremendous amount of indoctrination and organizational machinery is called for. Since it is difficult for one person to tell another how much he ought to give to the church, the impersonal authority of the Bible is utilized again and again in the material that goes forth. For example, in the November 29, 1959 issue of *The First Baptist Herald,* nineteen Scriptural quotations were presented to give the tithe this divine authority. Frequently denominational or interdenominational departments will aid the local church in producing publicity and training in organizational mechanics to get off a good campaign.

This does not necessarily mean that the minister will not lend his personal authority to the cause of raising the annual budget. Even though this is one of the more delicate areas, the ministers of the Bay Area would frequently use strong words in pulpit and print to obtain the necessary financial support for the church. Below, a minister couples personal and Scriptural authority to meet these needs.

One of our good members handed me a report from a church in which she and her husband had been members. They, too, were having financial problems. . . . Another of our members back from an extended vacation with a similar report . . . *but,* this does not help us meet our needs. . . .

It is not a question of any of us being out of work. God has blessed us wonderfully. It is a question of doing our share with what he has given us. Someday, we are going to have to give an accounting of our stewardship and we will want some better excuse than we have right now for spending his money on ourselves.

What is the answer?? *Tithe!* In the Old Testament we find
"tithing" commanded. In the New Testament, we find it commanded by Jesus. His call is for our heart and soul and the only
acceptable gift is ourselves.

The tithe is a minimum standard—a starting point for our
giving. No longer under obligation, we should exceed the old
obligation.[10]

Value infusion and internal stratification. Every social
group develops its peculiar stratification of roles, and the religious institution is no exception, even in its smallest units.
This system of internal stratification is recognized and utilized
in the church through various means of granting prestige,
privilege, and authority. Perhaps ordination is the most widely
known.

At the top of the stratification system in the local church is
the senior minister who has authority in administering the
sacraments, leading in worship, and presiding at "official
board" meetings, although authority and function will vary
somewhat with denominations. Distinctive vestments, rituals,
and titles commonly lend their authority to the office of the
clergy.

But the stratification system does not stop at this point.
Considerable prestige, if not authority, is granted the laymen
in the organizational structure, and where this is felt to be
significant it serves to ease the recruitment problem for these
offices. Thus, among the Presbyterians there is an ordination
of "ruling elders" (laymen). At the high moment in the special
order of service for this purpose the minister of the church
lays his hands on the heads of the elders to be ordained and
says:

> Set apart, O Lord, these thy servants, to the work whereunto they
> have been called by the voice of the church. Endue them plen-
> teously with heavenly wisdom. Grant them thy grace, that they
> may be good men, full of the Holy Spirit and of faith, ruling
> in the fear of God. Give them that favor and influence with the
> people which come from following Christ. So fill them with his

Spirit that they may lead this congregation in his service. Make them faithful unto death, and when the Chief Shepherd shall appear, may they receive a crown of glory that fadeth not away. Amen.[11]

Installation services are also used in abundance in the church, and at the time of the year when church offices are regularly changed, the clergy find themselves performing numerous installation services for the various organizations of the church. In passing, it should not be overlooked that the leaders of the various groups in a church most frequently think of themselves as "officers" rather than "teachers." In answer to the question, "What is your relationship to the group?" the seventy-four persons who responded to the leadership questionnaire in the nine Bay Area churches categorized themselves as follows:

Officers	56
Teachers	12
Other	6
Total	74

A further indication of the marginality of teachers in the stratification system of the local church is the fact that installation services for the Sunday morning church school staff (unavoidably labeled "teachers") are rarely utilized in the local churches. Most of the denominational books of ritual do not include such a service of installation. But perhaps the expressions of the laity are still more revealing of the status of the teacher in the local church. In the minds of most laymen one becomes an honored "pillar of the church" when placed on the "official board" but gets "stuck" with a teaching job in the church.

The stratification system of the local church, as in any other organization, is a system of granting prestige, privilege, and authority to the specific offices and roles that are necessary to its daily existence. It is especially necessary for an organization that must rely upon a voluntary incentive system for participation and co-operation. For this reason the stratification system is usually the object of much value infusion. It should not go without our notice, however, that the teaching staff of the church is expected to give considerable time and energy but receive little status and authority.

INSTITUTIONAL SUPPORT THROUGH PERSONAL SATISFACTIONS

Not all the values that sustain the religious institution come from the presentation of the distinctively religious rationale. Much of the value comes from a heavy yield of personal satisfactions in small groups where primary relations frequently develop and a process of socialization builds associational solidarity. In the church, where religious values have grown precarious and contributed to the marginality of the religious enterprise (see Chapter III), the selective recruitment of participants for the development of numerous small groups (see Chapter II) has provided a rich source of personal satisfactions for institutional security in a changing culture.

Emergence of informal structures. One of the characteristics of the local church is that the formal structure is sufficiently limited to allow for an abundance of informal patterns to arise out of the spontaneous interaction of personalities and groups within the organization.[12] Selznick has stated that "an organization's informal structure is made up of those patterns which arise when the participants face persistent problems that are not provided for by the formal system." He explains that these problems arise out of the impersonality, lag, and generality of the formal system, plus personal problems and interests.[13] In the church these sources of informal structure are accented.

As pointed out previously, the vagueness of the institutional purpose and the diffuseness of organizational goals provide considerable range to activities that come under the jurisdiction of the church.[14] Such generality makes it easier for the religious institution to adapt to changing conditions and changing interests of the participants. Over the years, some organizations in a church will fade away and others will emerge. The constant rotation of people in and out of the groups of the church spawns new and changing interpersonal relationships that may give rise to changes in the formal structure as well as initiate a host of informal activities.

The church's volunteer system also makes it necessary to reach individuals as persons if the incentive system is to be adequate. Many church leaders go beyond the normal interest in an individual when a task is to be performed. Knowing churchmen know the value of "personal contact" in providing motivation for the otherwise impersonal, technical, task-oriented formal system.

Furthermore, the volunteer incentive system of the church does not provide for full-time officials, serving over an extended period of time, but, rather, volunteers who give but a fraction of their time to the religious enterprise, change frequently in their posts, and embody a variety of motivational patterns. Under such a system the development of a formal system is dwarfed, the span of control[15] is greatly limited, extensive delegation of authority is necessary, and central authority is weak. Consequently there is great leeway in the development of informal structures where formal structures are immature. This freedom nourishes many informal structures in "natural" situations for any who allow themselves "churchly" interests beyond the formal Sunday morning worship service. As previously mentioned almost every group in the church provides opportunities for purely social interest. In fact, this occupies so much of the time and energy of many church groups that one would naturally assume that this is their dominant purpose. When seventy-four group leaders were asked "What social activities has your group had in the last twelve months?" they reported the affairs listed in Table 19.

TABLE 19

Social Activities of Adult Church Groups

Type of Activity	Frequency
Dinners, luncheons, teas, etc.	52
Parties	47
Picnics	19
Excursions	5
Retreats	5
Films	2

Source: Seventy-four adult group leaders responding to a questionnaire in nine Bay Area churches.

Hence, in a host of social situations—classes, committees, parties, dinners, teas—informal structures are constantly encouraged and come to characterize much of the activity in the orbit of the church. As a consequence, friendships, cliques, and interest groups emerge.

Personal satisfactions in primary relations. Because of the lack of tightly reined formal structures in the local church and the set of institutional characteristics that limit their development, it is not surprising that the local church is a breeding ground for primary relations. Primary relations embody (1) response to whole persons rather than segments, (2) communication that is deep and extensive, and (3) personal satisfactions that are considered paramount.[16] When such characteristics are embodied in a group, that group is considered a primary group. Such groups are readily found in the local church.

When Charles Horton Cooley first identified the primary group, he referred to it as the "nursery of human nature"[17] because of its importance to the individual's developing personality and social values. The need and the desire of an individual for primary group experiences has long been recognized and even used as a means of social control. The primary group is the main link between the individual and society that begins with the family and extends out and beyond this restricted world to the factory, neighborhood, army, church, and other associations. Although the individual-sustaining functions of the primary group are not fully understood, the following elements are undoubtedly present:

1. The primary relation is the area where *uniqueness* counts. Here the individual gains a sense of being accepted and wanted for himself. He does not need continuously to prove himself.

2. From his primary group membership the individual derives an image of himself; his continued membership in the group sustains that identity. When the "sharp dresser" or the "big wheel" or "Joe's pal" moves to a new environment, he must re-establish his identity, or find a new one, sometimes under great difficulties. . . .

3. Because the primary group takes account of the whole person, knowing him and adapting to his many individual characteristics, it can soften the impact of externally imposed rules and regulations. *The primary group protects the individual by reinterpreting and modifying goals and rules, and by adapting them to the capacities of the individual and to his special personal circumstances.*[18]

One young adult, who had obviously been accepted by her group and had experienced numerous primary relations, enthusiastically reported on an association that held many social satisfactions for her.

It's the friendliest church group that I've ever been in. They ask you to do things right off instead of treating you like a stranger for months and months. They helped us (several girls who lived together) to move and that was a real surprise. . . . They helped us to find this apartment, too. All we had to do was to mention that we were looking for a little bigger place and we had dozens of people looking for us.[19]

Frequently such social experiences will move a person to church affiliation when the religious motivation will not be sufficient to get him out of bed on Sunday morning or turn his head from the television in the evening. Unfortunately we do not have enough research at the present time to speak quantitatively about the pulling power of social satisfactions as over against the purely religious ones. We can be certain, nevertheless, that the pulling power of purely social activity is considerable.

Personal satisfactions in socialization. The churchmen among the readers of this work have undoubtedly been exposed to numerous statements concerning the "presbyterian form of church government," "the Methodist connectional system," or "the freedom of the Baptists" depending upon their religious affiliation. Whether the actual facts support great differences between religious systems and beliefs or not, a person is not a member very long before he begins to accept the idea that there is something unique about the values of a particular system of belief or polity. Churchmen become proud of the fact that they are either Presbyterians, Methodists, Baptists, or are of some other religious identity, and the old refrain "I'm a Methodist till I die" is frequently more than a fiction set to music. It was not by chance that Dr. C. O. Johnson was frequently billed "Mr. Baptist" when he spoke in the Baptist churches of the Bay Area.[20] Dr. Johnson had so internalized the Baptist point of view and worked so hard in Baptist activities that he had won this envied label among fellow Baptists.

This process of building group values and key attitudes into the individual is called *socialization*. "Socialization tends to be great when an organization needs to reshape its human materials."[21] The church receives its members from a heterogeneous society where other processes of socialization go on in the family, on the job, and in distinctive pockets of "culture" throughout our pluralistic society. When an individual identifies with another church or makes his way to the church from a highly secular orientation, it is advantageous to the church that he assumes the "decisional premises" of the newly found institution. This will ordinarily take place as the newcomer participates in the array of social roles and situations.

One of the main objectives of Chapter III was to illustrate how an individual tends to relate himself to a church where such "internalization of influence"[22] can be taken with greatest ease. When the situation is too demanding, participation lags and perhaps even terminates. Factors that make for a selective recruitment of religious participants serve to ease the process of socialization. If and when a person absorbs the general outlook of the organization and its distinctive approach to religion, the satisfactions that come through living and working with like-minded people are so valued that any threat to the institution becomes a threat to the individual. Socialization on this level is constantly taking place in the church and building a nuclear core of loyal personnel, as the following report reveals:

> If you had known the men from that class who are now on the Executive Board of the church when they first came to the class, you would not have believed the transformation. . . . The things you could hear them say after church out on the sidewalk would have shocked you to the core. It was just downright pagan! Life was just a battle to "clean up" financially, regardless of what it cost in human life. . . .
>
> But then a number of things took place. . . . One night —————————— (class member) was coming home and his car piled up on the tunnel. The steering column dug deep into his chest. . . . He hung there between life and death in the hospital with all that oxygen and equipment around the room. Any little thing would have kicked it one way or the other (illustrating with his finger). But the members of the class stood with him. We all visited him frequently and a couple of us with consistent regularity. He could not understand why we kept it up. Sometimes I would bring literature—Weatherhead's *Will of God*—which he still has.
>
> When he got back to the class I was there that first Sunday. That big, broad-shouldered hunk of man stood up and told us how much it meant to have a Christian fellowship stand beside him during those long weeks. He cried. . . . It did something

for him and it did something to the group. Those fellas have changed and the group has changed.[23]

This is the sort of religious experience that the church strives to bring about in its small groups. Involved in this report are primary experiences prompted by the informal structures that arose out of the "natural" situations in a young couples class. Besides the bonds of friendship that provided rich personal satisfactions there was a socialization of religious values that not only bound the group together but supported the church as an institution. As we shall see later, not all group experiences work out so ideally for the church, but even when the religious rationale fails to find expression in an internal satisfaction, the personal satisfactions usually help to maintain it as an organization. These satisfactions are instrumental in building the social base out of which institutional solidarity and security is realized.

INSTITUTIONAL SECURITY THROUGH INTERNAL ASSOCIATIONS

Participation preoccupation. When a person looks at the master calendar of any local church or the scheduled use of the kitchen, he might easily wonder whether the church operates a social hall, catering service, or both. Evening after evening the lights go on in some section of the church, and if not at the church, in the homes of the parishioners. A church school class could not be found in the nine churches of this study that did not have its social functions or make significant allowance for them in their meetings. The writer found many social groups that had little if any religious significance except the partial attendance of the members on Sunday morning. As we found above, meals, luncheons, teas, and parties in countless variety form the basis of many organizational functions. "Pick up your fork and follow me" seems to be the text of the contemporary church.

Why is there a countless round of monthly (sometimes

weekly) parties, picnics, and dinners, as well as baseball, basketball, and bowling in season? Most theological statements of the church will be hard pressed to explain them. Nor can all of them be found quickly by mapping the local church organization: it is necessary to spend some time in the church and in church groups before some of the social groupings can be identified. Yet the local church is honeycombed with a multitude of groups that give structure to a great deal of the activity. Some of the institution-sustaining values of the participant preoccupation are as follows:

1. Because there is common difficulty in personalizing the religious rationale and incentive system, the personal satisfactions of these individual-sustaining experiences make for institutional support. Frequently such groups will become so valued and internalized for members that any threat to the group or the local church will be met by loyal efforts that make for institutional security.

2. Such morale-relevant centers of energy are potential sources of goal accomplishment. They make is possible for the local church to mobilize members and direct their efforts into acceptable channels. The stronger the personal satisfactions the more potential the local church has to exploit.

3. It is also true that involvement opens up new lines of communication through friendships and cliques. The sheer impossibility of the small professional staff to make all the personal contacts and communicate the bare essentials is obvious. These friendships make it possible for the individual to absorb many of the "decisional premises" and general outlook of the local church. In brief, they are added facilities in the constant demand for organizational outreach.

4. The building of a socially homogeneous base through internal groups enhances the delegation of authority and control in the decentralized local church. Limitations do not have to be spelled out in detail because the process of socialization disperses key attitudes and makes them personally relevant. The background and intent of the local church is "filled in" for

the newcomer without a great deal of intensive indoctrination. Since the span of formal control quickly dissipates in a voluntary organization such as the church, informal controls serve to supplement the formal mechanism when decisional premises are adequately disseminated. To put it in other words, the socialization that takes place builds the informal "frame of reference" as an extension of normal mechanisms.

The degree to which factors such as these are understood by the leadership in the local church varies from person to person. The degree to which they can be utilized by the clergyman often is as vital to his success in the church as his preaching or priestly abilities. Fortunate is the clergyman who can see natural situations emerging that can be turned into organizational structures. Still more fortunate is the clergyman who can identify the lay leaders who can motivate and guide new groups. Greatly "blessed" is the clergyman who can motivate the potential leadership when he finds it. Such a participation-protagonist can assuredly win out over the hairsplitting theologian whose trained incapacity calls for considerable organizational "savvy" when on the field.

"Deployable saints." A church does not become a beehive of interacting participants unless there is a mobile core of lay leaders who can convene, organize, and administrate the internal groups, as well as provide some direction for the total enterprise. Every clergyman is on the lookout for potential leaders and is reluctant to lose them to other churches or see them lapse into indifference. The life of the religious organization is dependent upon a nuclear core of lay leaders for the maintenance of its internal groups.

Some of these leaders come to the church from other local churches and are directed into responsible positions because of their capacities, training, and experience in other situations. However, few local churches can subsist on the leadership that other churches feed them, and it therefore becomes the perpetual task of the church to recruit leadership from the rank-and-file membership. As stated above, necessity of the church to recruit members has tended toward the merchandising of religion in a society that shops for religious satisfactions the way it shops for other commodities. To a great extent the local church survives by providing the "brand" or religious satisfactions that satisfy a particular public. Thus, when the religious clientele is attracted to the church it is for affiliation. This is accomplished through an ideological appeal that often involves some form of religious "excitement." But for purposes of leadership development and deployment this motivation must be redirected toward service functions. One might say that the ultimate organizational objective of the church is to transform secular society into the "holy city of God" through the transformation and mobilization of a responsible, committed core of deployable leaders who inspire, order, and direct the members of the religious community. In brief, religious satisfaction must be transformed from "consumption" to "production." This is no small task.

Who are these leaders in the "deployable core" of the local church? Where have they come from? What characteristics of these "foremen" and "supervisors" impinge upon the organizational character of the local church? Five factors can be profitably emphasized.

1. They are recruited from the homogeneous social base. In Chapter III we found that a process of selective screening through a succession of exposures to the religious community determines the social base of the local church. Those who come to leadership positions in their groups and within the church have been found compatible with the social milieu in which they abide. Although they have some distinctive qualities that enable them to stand out among their peers and find support for their leadership roles, they are able to speak the language of their peers and be sensitive to a common body of shared values and attitudes. They are unlikely to be radical or divisive within the group. Instead, the emphasis of common values and attitudes enhances group cohesion and supports the leader's status.

2. On the whole, local leaders are the product of a "natural" stratification system. Although this would not apply to the key administrative posts of the church as much as it does to the classes and social groups, the leadership emerges from the internal groups and is then "raised" to responsible positions by the groups themselves with the frequent sanction and occasional assistance of the clergy. The organizational structure of the church takes on the character of the leadership that emerges, and the top leadership does its best to fit them for their positions in the religious institution. In the main, it is a case of allowing natural leaders to emerge and then doing the best that can be done to endow them with a religious rationale. Because local units do take on the character of their leadership, some churches insist that officers and teachers of church organizations be members. With this restriction some control of the character of the internal associations can be realized.

3. They are the nuclear members of the church; their participation in the life of the church is more frequent and they tend to have more than one leadership role. The seventy-four responding to the leadership questionnaire were also active in the following capacities:

Committees	33
Other educational staff roles	20
"Official board"	9
Group officer	4
Choir	3
Seminary intern program	2
Church visitation	2
Church hostess	1
Usher	1

Besides these local church responsibilities, eleven were active as laymen in denominational offices and sixteen in interdenominational offices. Thirty-one were active in civic organizations.

It should not escape observation that the leaders in the adult groups within the church are in constant exposure to other functions and functionaries as well as the institutional premises of the church. With this much interaction, frequently in small groups (committees in particular), the process of socialization makes for the internalization of common values and standards, and strong bonds of friendship are developed within the leadership core. These facts were brought out in the response to two questions in the leadership questionnaire. In answer to the question, "How often are you in contact with other leaders in the church?" the responses were as follows:

23   I am *very frequently* in contact with other leaders.
39   I am *fairly frequently* in contact with other leaders.
 3   I am *very seldom* in contact with other leaders.
 0   I am *never* in contact with other leaders.
———
65   Total respondents

With this much interaction one would expect that there would be little disagreement among them. This is indicated by the response to the question, "Are you in general agreement with the decisions and policies of the 'official board' (chief administrative body) of your local church?"

20   I *don't recall* any disagreements.
41   I *fairly seldom* disagree.
 3   I *very frequently* disagree.
 9   I *don't know enough* about the "official board" to answer this question.
———
73   Total respondents

With this much interaction, homogeneity, and compatibility, it is possible for most of the leaders to communicate the "mind of the church" on significant issues. This becomes a particularly valuable quality in a leader when he can speak for the top leadership to his peers and colleagues among the laity. If leaders among the lay group structure accept beliefs and patterns of action, then it is easier for the members of the groups to accept them.

4. Although they vary with the individual, there are significant limits within which a leader can give himself to the church. When a person has to earn a living and support a family these responsibilities will be given primary consideration and the person will be only segmentally related to the church, that is, he can give only a part of himself to the church. However, in the case of a retired person without substantial financial worries or an unemployed wife with an "empty nest," participation can come close to total involvement. Most churches have several of the latter type, but those with definite limits to their involvement are much more common. To the degree that there are other demands and interests that involve an individual there will be less assimilation of that person in the organizational structure. There will also be more outside frames of reference to impinge upon the religious rationale through segmental leadership, i.e., other institutions will be communicating their rationales and value systems. Hence there will be more to compete with the religious world and a tendency for the individual to be less committed to the religious institution.

5. Perhaps it should not be taken for granted that these adult group leaders are volunteers. Even guest speakers rarely get an honorarium and if they do it is small and usually intended only to cover expenses incurred. As illustrated above this means that a high infusion of value is necessary for both motivation and control, and since the volunteers are most frequently nonprofessionals they are often urged to attend training sessions. Much of the time the laity come from training sessions with more motivational dynamic than technical know-how.

Although we have termed these lay leaders "deployable saints," let us not assume that they are entirely "deployable" or necessarily "saints." Mecklin has pointed out that the "saint" as a cultural type is on the wane in our time,[24] and Chapter II spoke of the lack of depth in the religious sophistication of our time. Furthermore, the term "deployable" at least implies that a person goes and comes when directed. It implies that he can be used and manipulated as an agent by those who "call the shots." Let us take a look at some of the further limitations of such assumptions.

1. In the first place, a local church cannot afford to lose leaders indiscriminately. The clergy realize that they are the core of the organization, and the clergy will frequently take quite a bit from the leadership in order to retain them for the church. This is indicated by the fact that leadership is rarely deposed and seldom rebuffed. "Guiding" leaders is considered an art of social relations, and envied is the clergyman who can accomplish radical changes without an upheaval in leadership personnel. In fact, the leadership can not only drop out of special responsibilities but also transfer membership to another church with relative ease. This pattern of dependency upon lay leaders by the clergy limits the control that they have upon them.

2. Each of the denominations in this study has democratic forms of government inherent in its system in which groups of people (laymen included) have a voice in many of the major decisions. When a principle of group management is effective it is difficult for an organization to go to extremes. Many are the clergymen who breathe more easily and sleep more soundly after a congregational meeting.

3. Churchmen are living in an increasingly secular world where the religious institution has come more and more into a marginal position in contemporary society. Constant exposure to other systems makes control of the lay leadership more and more difficult. The values that are socialized among lay leaders may not have come from internal religious sources but from the outside secular world. The clergyman can frequently become "a voice crying in the wilderness" even though he be among his own flock. The local churches of the slow-

moving rural economy found it much easier to insulate affiliates from challenging systems of thought and practice.[25] One of the reasons why the church is losing the battle for the minds of men is because insulation is no longer possible.

4. Another area where the church is losing the battle of control and direction is in the *absorption* of the individual.[26] Absorption may be accomplished by organizational measures. The most obvious is the sheer volume of activity. Worship services, committee meetings, classes, dinners, and teas sometimes minimize the opportunities for disaffection because they leave little chance for thought beyond the moment. At first glance it might seem to most churchmen that the church is holding its own on this point, but even though it may be increasing the number of meetings the monopoly of leisure time no longer is enjoyed by the church. This is particularly the case on the West Coast where leisure-time activities can range from skin diving to skiing at the same time of the year. As such factors as automation give the American people more and more leisure a lesser percentage of the total hours will be relegated to the church.

5. Another limitation of control, which has frequently become an actual threat in the history of the church, is the potential possibility of the internal groups of a church becoming centers of power in themselves. The history of the church through the centuries is replete with examples of secession. The inauguration of many local churches has been prompted by groups of dissatisfied members who took themselves out of another church to have it the way they wanted it. Whenever a loosely reined organization of people expends energy to accomplish objectives, they have inherent within them the power to channel energy toward objectives incompatible with the mother institution. Such threats serve to limit the control of the "deployable saints."

6. The element of conservatism is also a restraint upon the control of group leaders. The church has been known for its conservatism in many areas and this characteristic is an ex-

pected element in the development of institutionalization.[27] In this respect the church is caught in its own web. As we have seen above, it is necessary for the church to infuse its organization with value. This must be done in order to sustain interest over an extended period of time amid conflicting ideologies, and to weld together a social collective into a homogeneous community pursuing specific objectives.

The process of development and transmission of self-images is useful but potentially frustrating. A church frequently finds that in one period it has developed a body of "understood" meanings that must be necessarily altered in another era in order to have an adaptive, viable institution. Such a body of shared beliefs or patterns of behavior may be a tremendous aid to communication in one period but a liability in the next. For example, when the home base of a local church has been secured financially and building debts are well in hand, a mission-minded leadership might infuse the values of foreign missions into the local church and develop considerable support for the outreach of the world mission within the local church. However, when it comes time for the local church to relocate or build on its own it becomes difficult for the local church to redirect funds to support its local needs. Certain portions of its regular offerings are committed, and wills are made out to support benevolent enterprises. Therefore, an enormous amount of energy must be expended in re-education before the standards and patterns of one age can be put aside and the new patterns inaugurated. This is especially true when specific aims and procedures have gained long-standing acceptance. In this fashion the conservatism of the church frequently limits the freedom of the leadership to deploy its resources, personal and nonpersonal, and to adapt to new demands.

Chapter VI

ADMINISTRATIVE INVOLVEMENT
OF THE MINISTER

THE PREVIOUS chapter has undoubtedly given the reader a picture of an other-directed organization both in recruitment and leadership deployment that develops certain mechanisms and strategies to deal with its insecurities. We have also seen that the church must adapt to the social environment if participation in the religious enterprise is to be won. Perhaps we have gained a better understanding of the frustrations of the professional leadership of the church in working with the laity. The layman comes "off the street," where he has been exposed to numerous frames of reference other than the religious, to take his place, if he can be so motivated, in the church with its own distinctive institutional premises. Furthermore, a major portion of the religious community never becomes sufficiently involved in the life of the church so that it accepts its distinctive premises. Through indifference, purposeful recalcitrance, lack of program and financial support, the laymen embody an informal, passive power factor that must constantly be appraised and acknowledged by the clergy and other key power figures in the church.

Nevertheless, the clergyman in the local parish has considerable power and authority in his role to compensate for the leverage of the laity. The overarching characteristic of the clergyman's role is the extent of his involvement in every phase of institutional life. In the multiphasic outreach of his role he is involved in almost every area beyond the level of the layman. Now we shall take a look at some further characteristics of this role to accent the manner in which such extensive involvement in a voluntary institution provides the clergyman with mechanisms of control and security not available to the laity.

Involvement in institutional premises.   The parish minister as the central actor (in the sociological sense) of the local church is involved in a social system oriented to a theological perspective. So long as the theological distinctiveness of the religious institution is accepted, the clergyman stands head and shoulders above all the other actors in the local church and maintains an authoritative position by virtue of his own extensive professional training. It is commonly expected that the clergyman know his church doctrine, church history, Bible, and the theological rationale for his priestly and prophetic functions. Even among the clergymen themselves there is frequently a certain aura of respect for the colleague who can drop an appropriate comment by Kierkegaard, Brunner, Tillich, or some other currently appreciated theologian. To be sure, a clergyman's theological sophistication frequently wears thin through the years of attending to the administrative requirements of his role, but at least he enters his profession with considerable exposure to the ideological rationale of the religious enterprise.

It is also important to keep in mind that a geographically decentralized enterprise in an increasingly secular culture requires a concentrated period of training for its "agents." States Philip Selznick: "Decentralization requires a preparatory period of training in which leadership has the opportunity to influence deeply the ideas that guide decision-making at lower levels. This influence may take the form of indoctrination, including the informal promotion of an official philosophy or even formal schooling."[1]

There is no doubt that the indoctrination of the institutional premises begins long before the future clergyman comes to a seminary. In most situations he has been raised within the religious community where many of the institutional values and behavior patterns have already been internalized. Often, though with increasing infrequency, the pretheological training was received in a church-related college where a religious climate had become a part of the institution. Nevertheless, the most significant exposure and involvement in the religious rationale comes during the seminary years in an atmosphere of relative isolation and extensive indoctrination. The future clergyman lives in a relatively small academic community of between one and two hundred students (there are few seminaries of more than three hundred students) that provides an abundance of small groups, and a familial-type climate that aids in the socialization of the institutional rationale prior to assignment in the local parish.

But even such a period of extensive indoctrination is not sufficient to maintain the leadership and secure its rationale when there is such a widespread geographical dispersal of local churches. The church follows its clergyman with conferences, retreats, workshops, institutes, and all manner of assemblages. Through such convocations the clergyman keeps up with the changing rationale of the religious institution and frequently returns to his field of labor with renewed enthusiasm for his calling. The seminary faculties frequently provide leadership for such "on the job" training, as do denominational leaders.

Furthermore, the co-optative tentacles of the religious institution relate the clergyman, almost without exception, to the denominational structures through a maze of committees and subcommittees, boards and other bodies necessary to carry on the work of the denomination at every level. These associations function to enhance institutional identification. The clergyman is now not only the mouthpiece of the institution—he *is* the institution. As a "company man" he can now be counted on to come through for the institution wherever he serves. A "crack" at the church now becomes a crack at the clergyman.

This was illustrated in one of the Bay Area churches where an extended discussion ranged over the topic of allocating a special amount of money to a local university program in Berkeley. The moderator (clergyman) of the "official board" argued that any money so designated should be sent "through channels." Members of the board insisted that when this was done it provided no "special" fund for the dispersal of this student foundation because it just became a part of the budgeted amount that the denomination designated to the foundation. The moderator, who had served as a member of numerous denominational committees and on a national mission board knew well the budget difficulties of designated funds when some kind of over-all equity for various programs had to be provided.[2] (For example, some persuasive leader from a mission field might come back on furlough and speak so convincingly of his particular field that a flood of specially designated gifts are received over a short period of time, and so upset the benevolence-supported programs of the church.) Although in this case the moderator was hard pressed to convince his knowing board members, he, like many of his colleagues, would speak for the decisional premises of his denomination because he had "become" the institution.

In such ways as these, clergymen are involved in the institutional premises upon which the work of the local church, as well as the denomination, are formed. They have spent considerable time in seminary and in "on the job" situations to acquire the rationale of the religious institution. Whether it is theology, polity, Scriptural authority, or explanations of the denominational bureaucracy that call for interpretation, the clergyman is the best qualified because of his extensive involvement. Frequently a layman might qualify in some area, but seldom does any layman come close to the total scope of the clergyman's understanding.

Involvement in incentive systems.   In order to understand some of the distinctive characteristics of the local parish it is necessary to ground our considerations in a number of observations concerning motivational patterns. Of course, no thorough description of the incentive system is presented here. The purpose is to identify certain distinctive incentive patterns that have become institutionalized and to describe the significance of each upon the character of the local unit.

In the first place it should be admitted that the clergyman has a tremendous stake in the role that he plays. He has more to lose than any other person in the local church and this involves both his professional status and his livelihood. Because of these potential costs to his career and his personal security the clergyman is prepared to exert significant amounts of time and energy to gain objectives and maintain control that a volunteer churchman is not prepared to render. The layman can "take it or leave it" when situations become frustrating, but the clergyman must stick with most situations until he has "outperformed" his opposition or motivated a congregation until the desired goals are accomplished.

There is also a further precariousness about the role of the clergyman in the local church. As pointed out in Chapter IV the control of the local clergyman is shared by the denominational hierarchy and the local congregation. For placement in local churches the clergyman is increasingly dependent upon denominational officials, but the local church (the source of his salary) can dismiss a clergyman almost at will in each denomination. Such a dilemma requires that the clergyman develop a schizophrenic orientation to the power structures that are not easily lived with. On the one hand, there is pressure from denominational officials, and at the same time the clergyman must deal with the recalcitrance of the parish members in expediting such programs through raising budget, recruiting workers, and administering program, while they hold the handle to the pay cup and can effect dismissal. If the clergyman gets his walking papers, it may not merely mean that his salary is curtailed by the local church but that he may have failed in accomplishing certain necessary objectives to implement denominational policy. Such artlessness reflects upon the professional ability of the clergyman and influences his opportunities to pursue his career. Thus it is that the local clergyman has much at stake in a precarious situation.

It should not be surprising then to find that the clergyman must spend a great deal of energy and time at his role if he is to handle it effectively. In such full-time concern he gains back a great deal of the advantage over the layman in administrative problems. The layman, because he spends such a brief time in office, seldom comprehends the formal and informal mechanisms of administration. Frequently laymen have reported that their first term on an "official board" or significant committee was spent in "learning the ropes." The functions of various administrative units have to be learned; channels of communication have to be discovered; and personalities in office have to be appraised before much can be accomplished by the layman. Frequently a layman will come on a board or committee without much sophistication about rules of parliamentary procedure or acquired skills in using such information. What he learns must be done on a part-time basis while the clergyman goes from meeting to meeting constantly utilizing these techniques. The experienced clergyman will utilize this leverage in meeting after meeting in such fashion that the opposing interests frequently become tactfully "sterilized" or impotent.

A further advantage to the clergyman is that he has a greater knowledge of the leadership pool that emerges in a church and has a hand in bringing potential leaders to the fore. The opportunity to suggest a leader or officer (in some cases the minister is an ex-officio member of the nomination committee) for a group is very common. This, of course, is a further leverage of considerable importance, for if a clergyman can surround himself with a small coterie of sympathetic and loyal laymen he can secure his situation and his program.

This can be best observed in congregational meetings by merely listing the persons who initiate the motions that come to the floor. The writer recently attended a congregational meeting where every motion and its second came from a member of the "official board" of the church. Since all the spadework in preparation for the meeting had been handled by the elders and the moderator, the rank and file had little comprehension of the issues at stake.

Such situations as this take place in the church because of the lack of involvement upon the part of the membership, as contrasted to the clergyman's extensive involvement in all its details, including the selection of the loyal nuclear core and its indoctrination. From the point of view of the leadership there is a sense in which lack of membership involvement serves a significant function. As a result there emerges in the local church a sort of "institutionalized *anomie*"[3] which appears necessary for the clerical control of different situations. The inability to decipher the complexities of the local church by the membership makes it possible for a matrix of informal structures to emerge where decisions are made and strategies projected. In such fashion the real authorities are veiled, meetings are packed, channels are bypassed, and considerable forethought can be given to the best way to present an issue when it must be subjected to a larger constituency.

Involvement in communication. Previously we have described some of the processes by which both formal and informal communication takes place through group structures of the church. Through the socialization that takes place in these subgroups of the local church a distinctive social base emerges and through the establishment of primary relationships, barriers to communication are broken down, formal rules are adapted to the individual situation, and the incentive system receives support from sources other than the strictly religious values. Although the development of such sources of institutionalization serve to enhance the communication system of the church and to render security through common loyalties and understandings, these groupings within the local church also serve as potential threats to organizational solidarity. What they can do for the support of the local church they can also do for the support of other endeavors not in keeping with the institution's self-interests.

Frequently there will be groups that cannot be motivated to develop any support or loyalty to the local church because the subgroup becomes an entity in itself. In many situations, groups within the church cannot be persuaded to take on significant services to the parent institution. No church maintenance projects are undertaken, no dinners are served, no benevolent projects are supported! What bothers clergymen even more is that many subgroups lose their distinctive character as religious bodies. Such problems were common in the churches of the Bay Area.

But perhaps the greatest threat is the recurring phenomenon of splinter groups that spring from a local church over "fundamentalistic doctrines or administrative grievances that have found harbor in the small group. Since there is so little control to exert in keeping an individual or a group of people within the local church, it is easy for this potential source of energy to move itself, and perhaps some others also, into an alignment with some other religious institution.

To meet dangers such as these and other threats to the administrative goals of the local church, the clergyman has a number of mechanisms that aid his interests. Although the pulpit is not without its significance, more important is the fact that the clergyman stands at the hub of communication in the church throughout the week. All major communications pass through his hands, and most are directed to him. Thus, he takes his position at the nerve center of the local organization and has daily opportunities to feel the pulse of the entire congregation in a way that no other person can. Most of the contacts he makes with people are informal and some of them confidential. The interests, problems, personality quirks, and capacities both potential and realized come before him with such frequency in daily encounters that nobody stands in a better position to appraise and direct the congregation. As the minister works with the problems of administration, certain individuals are brought to the fore and others are eased out, some persons are ignored in their complaints and others set the machinery in operation, some are directed to the "proper channels," and other persons set informal communication in motion.

But not all communication takes place through face-to-face relationships. The church office is where most of the written communication originates. Here it is selectively designed to accomplish certain objectives. It goes out in the form of parish papers, letters, fliers, tracts, memos, and periodicals of various quality and format. The person who initiates, edits, or censors the communication systems in any organization has strategic tools in his hands to modify and control the behavior of the enterprise. Not only is it important to control the production of written and oral communication, but it is also necessary to handle what is received with discretion. The church staff will frequently find it profitable to "filter" the communication that it receives as it passes it on. Sometimes it is appropriate to accent the "spirit" of the correspondence rather than the precise wording and vice versa. Sometimes it is appropriate to funnel correspondence quickly to the appropriate committee and at other times to delay the delivery of correspondence.

Another example of utilizing the communication center as a means of control was noticeable in one church which required that all items for the agenda of the "official board" be funneled to the church in advance so that the agenda might be distributed to board members for adoption at the meeting. Not incidental to the value of such a strategy is the fact that there is ample preparation for what may come before the board and insulation against surprise propositions from the floor. But even without this administrative mechanism it is apparent that clergymen do come prepared for the "hot" issues. Complained one board member, "_____ (minister) is an effective speaker and he gave the board the idea that this was the Christian action to take. After he made his speech it appeared that we were voting for or against sin."[4]

Involvement in authority structure. A further necessity of the clergyman in a local church is the establishment of an authoritative base from which he can work within the parish to effectively administer his local unit. The novice might easily assume that the clergyman has all the authority that is necessary by virtue of the fact of his "call," or his ordination, or the powers vested in the office through the distinctive polity of the denomination. Although the clergyman will not discount any of these factors that may stand in his favor, they are far from adequate when any major adjustment in the life of the church is called for. On the contrary, it is a commonly accepted dictum among the clergy that no basic changes ought to be attempted in the first year of office in a new church. Many will advocate an even longer period before the clergyman can be sure that his authority is secure enough to venture into some radical readjustment in the reconstruction of a parish. Such commonly acknowledged facts must indicate that something important must transpire before significant changes can be realized. We shall see that part of what takes place is the laying of an authority base as the launching pad of institutional innovations.

That authority does not transfer with the transfer of local church leadership can be seen from the definitions of power and authority. Power signifies the ability to carry out one's will *despite the inertia or resistance of others.*[5] Power is the predisposition or prior capacity that makes the influence or control of the actions of others possible even though there is no institutional sanction for this control. Power is necessary to support "the fundamental order of society and the social organization within it, wherever there is order. Without power there is no organization and without power there is no order."[6]

Authority is defined as formalized or *institutionally recognized* power. "Authority is thus the expected and legitimate possession of power."[7] Thus authority must be *officially legitimated* and *voluntarily accepted* by the group. Simon stated it nicely in the following paragraph:

> The relationship of authority can be defined, therefore, in purely objective and behavioristic terms. It involves behaviors on the part of *both superior and subordinate*. When, and only when, these behaviors occur does a relationship of authority exist between the two persons involved. When the behaviors do not occur there is no authority, whatever may be the "paper" theory of organization.[8]

Even though it takes time to establish the clergyman's authority, it should not be assumed that he enters the local church bare. He comes to the church as the church's ordained "man of God." He will be referred to as "the Rev. Mr. _____" or some modification of this phrase of deference. In many situations he will be installed in an impressive ceremony in which the local clergyman will "borrow" status from the denominational officials who take part. Usually he will wear distinctive vestments as symbols of his office.

Tradition will also help to establish his authority. He will be expected to lead the worship and in so doing be the "chief" priest among his congregation. The administrative structure will provide places for him to assume leadership roles. Sometimes his role will be supported by the more sacred traditions of the Holy Scriptures, and will stand in a *quasi-charismatic* succession.[9]

Other resources include such items as his intensive training for his role and the experience he has had in establishing himself in similar situations elsewhere. He will embody certain personality traits and a certain personal charisma that also may be utilized to undergird his bid as an authority figure within the church.

Paul M. Harrison[10] has done us a service in distinguishing between the *rational-legal* and the *rational-pragmatic* types of authority in the church. Validation of authority within the church is based on rational and legal grounds when the members of the religious community accept "belief in the 'legality' of patterns or normative rules and the right of those elevated to authority under those rules to issue commands."[11] This authority stems primarily from the occupation of the legally established office of the minister and not from any special attributes of his person.

On the other hand, the pragmatic authority is not undergirded by the legality of rules, but must be won by the clergyman through informal opportunities to gain power. This is possible because the clergyman is so thoroughly involved in the broad expanse of the administration of the local parish. He possesses opportunities to enhance the status of certain offices, to utilize the channels of communication to further specific objectives, to direct support to or withdraw support from certain personalities or pet projects, etc. The advantages that accrue to the clergyman because of his extensive involvement undergird the system of pragmatic authority and "fill in" where the traditional, legal, and charismatic sources are not adequate.

Of course, there is no magical formula for the clergyman to adopt in the building of authority. It will depend upon his own personal resources and the culture base with which he must identify. In some situations an informal first-name relationship will build the necessary acceptance, but in other situations this would be repulsive to the congregation. In some situations an emotion-laden sermon with a "gospel" message would establish the fact of the "call" of the minister, and in other congregations a straightforward analysis of a social problem from a Christian perspective by a well-read minister would clinch the clerical authority.

Hence, we are not ready to say precisely how the clergyman acquires the authority that he must gain in order to effectively administrate his local parish, for one would have to fill in more of the details with research and an elaboration of the situation. We can be certain that it is no insignificant task. It is also safe to say that each clergyman is on his own and must "sink or swim" largely by his own resources.

FUNCTIONAL PRIORITIES

In response to the pressures placed upon clergymen in recent times, seminaries have added many new courses and clergymen have been expected to gain competency in a number of specialized areas. Currently a "soul searching" process of self-assessment of seminaries is under way in which the many hats of the clergyman are being appraised as a guide to the restructuring of the seminary.[12] Samuel Blizzard's study of 1,111 college- and seminary-trained clergymen who minister to local churches in the continental United States has added significantly to the understanding of the local church as well as provided guidelines for the seminary.

One point of the Blizzard study of interest to us is its picture of the demanding time expenditure required of the clergyman. "The professional work day of the co-operating ministers averaged a few minutes less than ten hours (rural men worked nine hours and seventeen minutes: urban men worked ten hours and thirty-two minutes)."[13] This further accents the degree of involvement necessary for the administration of the local parish already discussed.

However, it is even more significant for our interest in adult education to follow the breakdown of ministerial roles into their various categories. According to the Blizzard survey, the average minister regards the preaching role as being of first importance, followed respectively by the roles of pastor, priest, organizer, administrator, and finally teacher.[14] It is interesting that in the minister's scale of priorities the teaching role is not highly valued. But, as Blizzard points out, more than a scale of priorities is necessary to explain the roles of the clergymen. The time that the clergyman spends on performing these roles is likewise a factor. The order from the most time-consuming to the least time-consuming is as follows: administrator, pastor, preacher and priest, organizer, and teacher. This led Dr. Blizzard to point out that the minister does not divide his time in accordance with his personal scale of values and preferences, but in accordance with the demands that are placed upon him. Ministers responded passively to the role expectations of the parishioners, the communities, and the program pressures of the denominational boards. In brief, this study revealed a great disparity between the importance and satisfaction assigned to respective roles and the *functional priorities* devoted to each.

Most significant of all to our interest in adult education is that *the teaching role ranked on the bottom in both importance and function.* Regardless of the lip service given to the teaching work of the church, this study reveals that when the minister is forced to rank teaching among other roles it comes out on the short end of things. Furthermore, when this study counted the time involvement of the clergyman, teaching again came out on the short end. According to Blizzard two thirds of the minister's day is spent as administrator, one fourth as pastor, one fifth as preacher and priest, one tenth as organizer, and the residue (about one twentieth) in teaching.[15] In the light of such statistics it does not appear that the church is ready to blossom forth with an expansive program of adult education.

As if this were not enough, David Ernsberger makes another significant interpretation of the Blizzard data which bears upon our concern. Next to the teacher, the "organizer" receives the least amount of time. As you may have noticed, Blizzard made a distinction between the organizer and the administrator. The organizer works with small groups of officers and program planners in directing the organizational life of the church. "Of all his major roles," states Ernsberger, "only the organizational and teaching roles involve the minister in work with *small primary groups* in the church."[16] In contrast to the small group, Blizzard had defined the administrative role as including all those functions which do not involve direct contact with parishioners. Concludes Ernsberger:

> Therefore the fact that the roles of organizer and teacher are regarded as least significant and satisfying, and receive the least amount of the minister's time, indicates that the primary or face-to-face group life of the church is minimized in favor of the ministry to individuals on the one hand and to the entire congregation on the other.[17]

Thus the roles of both teacher and organizer, the two most important roles in the development of an adult education program, are given the least opportunity to develop in the local parish.

INDICATIONS OF IRRATIONALITY[18]

In Chapter IV it was asserted that "the blurring of denominational distinctions has come about mainly through the adoption of bureaucratic characteristics common to all large-scale organizations in modern society."[19] Yet, in the same chapter certain resistances were indicated that check somewhat the rapid swing of the religious institution into the orbit of the rational pursuit of efficiency through bureaucratic procedures. It will be the thesis here that the local church is the weakest unit in the bureaucratic rationalization of the religious institution. It not only gives emphasis to familial, brotherhood, and democratic ideologies, but also embodies certain functional characteristics that make it difficult for denominational officials to deploy and manipulate rank-and-file churchmen.

Weak system of communication and control. One of the factors making for potential dissent is geographical decentralization. Rarely are great throngs of people assembled together under one roof in the church the way they are in a highly localized operation. The day-to-day business of the local church must take place where the people live and when access to them can be gained. This makes the local church a distinct type of unit with significant barriers to communication and with limited span of control.

Sheer distance alone makes impossible a great deal of inter-personal communication between the hierarchy and the rank-and-file members. Such a communication barrier makes it difficult to communicate the decisional premises of the upper echelons of the administrative hierarchy of the church to the local units. Therefore it is not surprising that the initiative for communication comes mainly from the headquarters staff in the form of conferences, workshops, retreats, etc., where the leadership of the local church can be exposed to administrative premises and objectives. The success of headquarters programs is not unrelated to the establishment of lines of communication with clergy and active laity in the local parish.

A further variable limiting the communication and control of denominational officials over the local church is that each of the local congregations differs in regard to the cultural base and concomitant religious attitudes as discussed in Chapter III. For example, the local church that tends to recruit its affiliates from the lower socioeconomic levels also tends to embody more sectlike religious attitudes.[20] Sect-type religious attitudes make it more difficult to accept denominational premises and programs pitched to a church-type orientation. Hence, promotional and curriculum materials as well as philosophies supporting them will be rejected occasionally by local churches because the sources of religious attitudes of local churches do not always support official philosophies and programs. A particular climate may persistently permeate a local situation in spite of the fact that the local clergyman may desire to pull it more in line with the denominational frame of reference.

Furthermore, church history is replete with examples of local churches that felt themselves so out of tune with the denominational premises that they have pulled out of the denomination entirely. Sometimes clergymen themselves have provided the leadership for the "colonizing" of those churches into separate, independent denominations. The *Yearbook of American Churches*[21] illustrates this, with the division of the Baptist churches into twenty-seven bodies, the Methodist into twenty-one bodies, and the Presbyterian into ten.

At headquarters centers of a denomination, the main characteristics of a bureaucratic structure can be provided and maintained much more easily than in the local unit. Here there are formal and informal mechanisms to deal with the recalcitrant or incapable official,[22] but in the local church such mechanisms must be more carefully appraised and tactfully carried out because of the dependency of the local leaders upon the membership. Alienating lay members depletes the leadership pool, cuts off financial support, lowers numerical statistics, and spreads dissatisfaction to other members.

The amount of energy that must be poured into local churches by the clerical leadership as described above is another indication that the control system is weak. When such overwhelming involvement with each and every phase of the religious operation is necessary to keep it secured, it indicates a serious degree of irrationality in the formal system of control. Although such a system may have its advantages in an associational society such as ours, it does imply limits upon the bureaucratic development of the religious enterprise.

A further indication of the weak system of control is the ease with which members can terminate their affiliation and transfer to another church. When an institution has such a tenuous hold upon its members and is so eager to acquire new members that its standards include almost everyone, it is not easy to deploy them to work for the institution when jobs may be frustrating, depressing, time-consuming, or of low status.

However, it should not go without notice that a long-term association with a local church is likely to produce numerous close associates, perhaps a position of esteem, and valued experiences in primary relations that are not easily laid aside. When the long-term association of the member has provided such personal satisfactions, he will weigh them against persistent problems and unpleasant associations of his work load.

Voluntary incentive economy. Another phase of institutional existence that makes for weakness in the rational pursuit of organizational objectives is the voluntary system of incentives upon which the local unit must depend. Most of these factors have been discussed elsewhere in this study, so extensive development is not needed here.

1. Participants in the religious enterprise are segmentally related to the church. By this is meant that they give only a minor portion of their time and energy to the church. It is not their vocation or profession and their livelihood is not dependent (at least directly) upon their affiliation with it. Frequently they are members of other organizations, and the church must share their loyalty. Seldom are the participants involved to the extent that they could not easily pull out and affiliate elsewhere. If a member had to stick with a local church regardless of its frustrations because he was economically dependent upon it, he would be more willing to make the best of the situation.

2. The amount of energy poured into the process of infusing the religious institution with value also reflects a weak incentive system. When the topics of sermons, discussions, workshops, conventions, seminars, retreats, and numerous other types of gatherings emphasize the religious character of the institutional church and the religious way of life, it would appear that such values must be meeting opposition in our increasingly secular age. When a broad variety of topics and types of program does *not* appear, it reflects the fact that the job of establishing the values of employment in the religious enterprise has not been adequately accomplished, so that the character of the religious institution might take on other objectives. This "obsessive" infusion of value that constantly takes place in the church reflects the incentive needs and problems.

3. The main exception to the process of infusing religious frames of reference into the religious institution is the tolerance of distinctively social programs. Such manifestations of church program are in evidence because of (a) the weak control system and/or (b) the realization that the personal satisfactions of purely social programs augment the religious satisfaction in the strengthening of the church. Undoubtedly both of these are explanations for this phenomenon in the churches. In the Bay Area churches some of the ministers lamented the proliferation of purely social programs but were unable to do much about them. Other clergymen offered little resistance because they felt it necessary to build the "fellowship."

4. The other-directed character of the recruitment enterprise of the church also indicates a certain irrationality in the handling of its internal affairs. It indicates a dependency upon "selling" participation in the religious institution rather than an impersonal development of affiliates. This is an emphasis upon "consumption" rather than "production." It reflects a spectator orientation of the public to the church.

5. The stratification system is not one that is established through a system of monetary rewards but one predicated upon prestige and status within the institution itself. It is dependent upon ritual, Biblical authority, and the "natural" ascendancy of leadership within the religious community. Although stratification systems undergirded by monetary rewards have long appreciated the social sources of incentive, the church must be dependent upon these alone. As a result lay ordinations and special installations have been accented in the religious institution.

6. Lastly, there is within every church a real shortage of leadership to accomplish the tasks that local churches face. This is especially true in the areas of educational leadership. Even to maintain the program of the church school requires a large and significant group of teaching and administrative

leadership. Rarely does one find a church that has sufficient staff to accomplish its objectives. This leadership problem is an everyday concern.

Churches as "cultural" associations. A distinction between *civilizational* and *cultural* interests is a useful one when applied to the religious institution if we can guard against the danger of blurring the inevitable causal linkage between the two. The last thing that the writer would like to convey is the idea that an organization can have its ultimate goals without concern for the instrumental methods. Nevertheless, Charles H. Page utilizes these concepts with profit.

These characteristics of bureaucracy—standardization, self-perpetuation, overformalism, and antipathy for the client—reach their fullest development in associations of a certain type: in others they may be found in only embryonic form. In the first class must be placed the grand-scale agencies organized to forward what certain writers have designated *civilizational* interests. These interests are predominantly instrumental; they are sought that men may realize further goals, or are pursued in order to establish material and social conditions within which the culturally defined "good life" may be led. This is the area in which the *secular* overshadows the *sacred;* in which those imposing institutions of technological, economic, and political design have mushroomed to huge bureaucratic proportions in recent time. Here bureaucracy is an apparatus functionally especially appropriate for the achievement of civilizational tasks; to produce economic goods and services, to run a complex fiscal system, to manufacture (though not to invent) atomic weapons, to conduct international trade—or international struggle—to man the garrison state. There are some dissenters as to the *human* appropriateness of bureaucracy in even these spheres, particularly among the decentralists such as Huxley and Mumford and Bertrand Russell, but the dissent is on the other than civilizational, i.e., instrumental, grounds.

This dissent, it should be stressed, is rooted in the second great class of interest, the *cultural:* and/or terminal values that define things as good (or bad) in themselves. While cultural interests are often found in the large civilizational agencies, most apparently in the case of the political state, in this area they are discouraged and, indeed, held in abeyance by bureaucracy itself. But in other organizations—educational, professional, scientific, recreational—the end values of culture are very much in the picture: they cannot be wholly overlooked for the sake of smoother operations and efficiency. Here the sacred, i.e., the culturally defined good, whether in the school or scholarly group or recreational organization, strives for at least equal status with the secular or instrumental. This is an important reason why bureaucracy, as a system of administrative control and procedure, is rarely so efficient, is rarely so fully grown, in the cultural organizations. And here, also, is an important reason why the "threat of bureaucracy" is a source of serious concern for those hard bent on making possible the realization of cultural interests. Both bureaucracy's inefficiency and its menace of efficiency and order are nowhere more apparent than in the cultural association of the nonauthoritarian church.[23]

The observation of Rankin, referred to in the preceding chapter, that the familylike, brotherhood quality and teaching of the church seems to be something of a defense against the bureaucratization of the church is not inappropriate to discussion of the cultural quality of the religious institution that Page has discerned. A group that has as its *raison d'être* the mystical experience, knowledge for its own sake, a simple fellowship, as well as the qualities that Rankin has identified in The Methodist Church, embodies a certain quality that characterizes it as a cultural type.

Page further maintains that if an association is to maintain its cultural character then it must embody two important principles: (1) it is "either itself a primary group or else a union of primary groups linked together by a central organization" and (2) "the liberty of alternatives, expressed, on the one hand, in the individual's freedom to elect and to follow those interests he finds significant and satisfying, and, on the other hand, in the organization's freedom to exist side by side with groups professing quite contrasting or even opposing doctrines."[24] In the first instance the group achieves its end through the *process* of meeting others, rather than through the creation of a *product* as is common in the civilizational association. In the latter instance the granting of full freedom in alternatives is not complementary to the criterion of efficiency that permeates the civilizational association but is appropriate in the cultural association where pluralism is allowed to exist in spite of its threatening consequences organizationally.

Further insights into the cultural quality of the religious institution are to be gained through an appreciation of the fact that there is in any local church a certain degree of sectness. By definition a sect-type religious institution renders support to the cultural irrationalities of the local church. Troeltsch has described them as follows:

> The sects, on the other hand, are comparatively small groups; they aspire after personal inward perfection, and they aim at a direct personal fellowship between the members of each group. From the very beginning, therefore they are forced to organize themselves in small groups, and to renounce the idea of dominating the world. Their attitude toward the world, the State, and Society may be indifferent, tolerant, or hostile, since they have no desire to control and incorporate these forms of social life; on the contrary, they tend to avoid them; their aim is usually either to tolerate their presence alongside of their own body, or even to replace these social institutions by their own society.[25]

This orientation of the sect-type religious expression to aspire after personal inward perfection and the renunciation of responsibilities in the world about them does not make for the forming of large mass organizations of bureaucrats. Qualities such as "personal achievement in ethics and in religion, the radical fellowship of love, religious equality and brotherly love, indifference toward the authority of the State and ruling classes, dislike of technical law and of the oath, the separation of the religious life from the economic struggle by means of the ideal of poverty and frugality, or occasionally in charity which becomes communism . . . the appeal of the New Testament and the Primitive Church,"[26] tend to emphasize the cultural rather than the civilizational interests.

Let us keep in mind that the church-sect typology is merely a heuristic conception and that religious institutions are not absolutely one or the other even though their tendencies may be pronounced. To the degree that the sect-type attitudes emerge in a religious institution there will be resistance to the bureaucratic rationalization of the local church to efficiently accomplish organizational objectives.

These complementary observations of Page, Rankin, and Troeltsch concerning what might well be designated the "cultural" (other wording might also be used) quality of the church must therefore be listed on the balance sheet opposite the growing tendencies of a bureaucratic rationale impinging upon the local church.

ADULT EDUCATION AND THE LOCAL CHURCH

These organizational characteristics of the local church are not unrelated to the past and future role of adult education within the church. Let us now appraise these characteristics of the local church as they condition the role of education couched within this organizational unit.

Potentials for broad educational pursuits. The term "broad educational pursuits" indicates program that is not necessarily limited to that which enhances institutional security. A number of factors indicated above may work beyond these limitations.

1. It is hoped that we have gained an appreciation of the local church as a distinctive type of organizational unit in the denominational organization of the religious enterprise. As such it is the weakest but perhaps most important link in a rational pursuit of efficiency via the bureaucratization of the religious institution. This inability of the local unit to rationally administrate its affairs limits the direction of the rank-and-file membership into types of organizational activity

designed mainly for institutional security and makes it possible for members to drift into other areas of concern, such as education. In brief, members cannot be limited to narrow areas of concern because officials will it. On the other hand, it is not implied that this will inevitably develop a broad adult education program. In fact, there is much evidence to support the observation that, when left without leadership with this interest, local church groups drift toward the purely social types of activity. When adult education does emerge it is a "low pressure" variety that makes little demand. The weak control of the rank-and-file members of the religious institution is a potential factor that could make for a broader range of adult education, but it has remained undeveloped because of the lack of concerted leadership.

2. Since recruitment needs so persuasively motivate the leadership of the local church toward increasing membership, these needs also become a potential source of initiative for adult education when such programs are interpreted as a medium of recruitment. For example, certain publics are attracted to forums on pertinent local, national, and international affairs. For some potential members such programs are a mark of progressive and aggressive leadership and make the sponsoring institution more attractive in their eyes. When local church leaders look at adult educational activities in this light there is potential for the development of such programs.

3. Because of the unusually large expenditure of energy which the local clergyman invests in the administration of the local church, the potential for adult education increases as the size of the staff increases. Adult education has its best chance for development in large churches with multiple staffs. When one clergyman has to cover the whole water front, even though he may have fewer persons in his parish, he is spread so thinly that the initiation of new program is rarely ventured. It was noticeable that the multiple-staffed Bay Area churches offered a greater range to their educational programs than the single-staffed churches.

4. When a theological position of the clerical leadership incorporates the concept that all of life is related to the religious rationale and that specific problems of our age need attention by churchmen, there is also a potential for the development of a broad range of educational interests. This, it ought to be observed, is not necessarily unrelated to institutional security since it represents the attempt of the church to control its environment.

5. The complementary observations of Page, Rankin, Troeltsch, and others concerning the "cultural" characteristics of the local church also throw light upon the potential for adult education in the church. Education shares a concern for the end values of the "good life," and as such has this in common with the "sacred" concerns of the religious institution.

Limitations for broad educational pursuits. The major weight of the observations in this chapter tend in the direction of the limitation of the broad educational pursuits. Such a conclusion is supported by the observations that follow.

1. The insecurities of the local church tend to restrict the development of a broad range of educational enterprises in favor of activities that help secure the local unit as a viable organization. Indications of insecurity have been emphasized by the recruitment obsession, the other-directed pattern of dependency, the constant necessity of a value infusion, the tremendous amount of energy that must be invested by the clergy, and the resistances to the rationalization of the local church among others. As long as the religious institution continues its trend toward marginality in contemporary society and embodies such organizational insecurities, the development of a broad and inclusive program of adult education is not likely to occur.

2. The infusion of value that naturally results as a reaction to institutional insecurities tends to characterize adult education in the church by emphases upon the distinctive competence of the religious institution, the distinctive qualities of

the religious life, the distinctive character of religious ideology, and the distinctive values of religious leadership. As such, adult education in the church tends to emphasize a "distinctive" type of education rather than giving emphasis to a wide range of educational pursuits. This is prompted by the character of the needs and problems of the religious organization. Under such conditions, education that motivates for participation and leadership is more highly prized than education for the sake of knowledge itself.

3. The concern for recruitment tends to socialize a priority of values and behavior patterns of the sanctuary as superior to those of the classroom. The tendency in the contemporary religious institution is toward a spectator, theater-type consumption of religious experiences. The other-directed dependency relationship of the local church leaders upon the rank-and-file members of the religious institution tends to make of them a "clientele" which "shops" for religious experiences and a distinctive type of public among the numerous mass movements of contemporary society. The massification, spectator, theater-type trend in contemporary religious institutions is not conducive to the requirements of an adequate educational program by any measure. In spite of the tendency of the contemporary religious institution toward the massification of its participants, curriculum materials continue to be based upon premises of small groups and their characteristics.

4. The "irrationality" of the local church places significant limitations upon the organization and administration of a broadly ranged program under the sponsorship of the church. While the observations of Page, Rankin, Troeltsch, and others concerning the "cultural" quality of the church has an ideological affinity for educational interests, it also places limitations in the way of rationally and efficiently administered organizational structures that may be utilized to promote adult education. When cultural interests render communication, authority, control, and other factors necessary to a ra-

tionally administered institution more difficult, then greater energy must be expended to accomplish these ends. With such limitations upon the administration of the local church there is a pronounced tendency to take care of the administrative necessities first and the educational "embellishments" later. Consequently a program of adult education does well if it comes out second best.

5. The weakness in the formal support of the local clergyman and the consequent dependence upon administration through informal mechanisms requires such an energy expenditure that the local clergyman ventures to add little to his administrative load through the addition of extra program. It might be stated that most local clergymen do not even have the time to contemplate it. The local clergyman, close kin to the "marginal man" of sociological theory,[27] so jealously guards his energy disbursement that the necessities of local administration and professional career tend to dominate his personal incentive priorities.

6. Further resistances are met in the conservative nature of the religious institution. Habits, values, vested interests, and other rigidities are noticeable in all old-line organizations that have "developed orderly, stable, socially integrating forms and structures out of unstable, loosely patterned, or merely technical types of action."[28] It reflects its own peculiar history, the groups that have been established, the personalities of the leadership, and the way it has adapted to its environment. This is why the Blizzard studies have done us a service in making the distinction between organization and administration. The management of existing programs and forms of behavior can be accomplished with relative ease when compared to organizing new program.

This can be illustrated with a brief reflection of what takes place when a new program is undertaken in the church. Assuming that there is a real need, there follows considerable infusion of value for the new program. Leadership frequently comes from the nuclear members already active in local church program who have vested interests in the established programs. All too often new organizational units designed to promote new programs are seen as threats to existing organizational units. For this reason new programs generally have a better chance of materializing when new leadership is discovered before existing units of the local church have absorbed them.

7. The internal stratification system of the local church also mediates against the development of educational program. This stratification system relegates the professional educator (director or minister of Christian education) to the role of specialist working in one of the tributaries (not the main stream) of the life of the church. Likewise the educator must build his program among the laity in a stratification system that mediates against program development. Teachers are "low men" on the totem pole in comparison with other leadership roles in the church. A layman will frequently become installed or ordained (as in the Presbyterian Church) to the high office of "official board" member or elder in the church, but get "stuck" with a teaching job in the church school. Yet the number of teachers and the energy expenditure required both go beyond that of the board members.

The import of such findings are of no small significance, for there is probably no work of the ministry around which there is so much confusion of values and rationale with actual behavior and function. In this area Blizzard has done one of the best jobs of piercing the fog that covers the discrepancy between the lip service that the church gives its educational ministries and the existential situation. Unfortunately such findings do not give much encouragement to educational objectives.

Thus, as one concentrates his attention upon the character-making influences and expression of the local church, he is forced to conclude that the indices do not seem to point to a broad and inclusive program of adult education under the sponsorship of the church. The needs and problems for which the local church must find solutions to keep it viable in a changing culture do not encourage any great enthusiasm for an expansive program of adult education.

Nevertheless, the local church is only one phase of the total picture that must be seen in relationship to the whole enterprise. The church is still debating vigorously its distinctive competence as a religious institution in the light of its environment. Adaptation and accommodation is an ongoing process and the pace with which modern society moves is tremendous. In due time all of these influences affect the sense of mission of the church and the embodiment of that mission. It is now time for us to pull together the separate thrusts of this study into a comprehensive whole to understand the role of adult education within the total enterprise.

Chapter VII

THE MISSION OF ADULT EDUCATION

THE CHURCH has always had to make some adjustment to the social setting in which it found itself, but keeping up with the rapid pace of changing social phenomena in recent times has been and continues to be an extremely demanding task for the church. We have had much to say about the contemporary social milieu and the place of the church within it. We have found that in spite of the contemporary "return to religion," which gains support from church membership statistics, church construction figures, the popularity of religious books, songs, and movies, the religion of the man on the street is "a mile wide and an inch deep."[1] The religious institution in America has been described as a marginal institution that calls few of the shots in contemporary culture, and it has become one of the weaker institutions among the stronger power centers of our pluralistic age.

No churchman, however naïve, can continue unaffected by the rapid transition of the contemporary age. With the shaking of foundations has come a renewed emphasis upon theological and Biblical studies. At Amsterdam the World Council of Churches met under the theme of "Man's Disorder and God's Design" (1948). At Evanston the World Council assembled under the banner of "The Christian Hope and the Task of the

Church" (1954). During the ensuing years, religious publications have been studded with such titles as *The Structure of the Divine Society*,[2] *The Witnessing Community*,[3] *The Church Redemptive*,[4] *The Nature of the Unity We Seek*,[5] *The Significance of the Church*,[6] *The Misunderstanding of the Church*,[7] *The Purpose of the Church and Its Ministry*,[8] *The Nature of the Church*,[9] to mention only a few contributions to the theological adjustment.

Self-assessment

The reason for this flood of literature dealing with the nature of the church and its relationship to changing culture is not difficult to understand. Even before the changes in the social structure are understood there is need for a coherent philosophy of the church and its mission. The flood of books from the pens of the most sophisticated are symptomatic of the general concern and activity throughout the religious institution. Such a reassessment would be prompted in any institution confronting similar dilemmas. What shall we *be?* What shall we *do?* These are the questions of the hour, and it takes a thoroughgoing discussion to find such answers and work them in at the grass roots of the enterprise. One of the reasons the theologian has become such a prominent figure in the religious institution today is because these are his questions. It has been the theologian more than any other religious leader to whom the church has looked to "specify and recast the general aims of (the church) so as to adapt them, without serious corruption, to the requirements of institutional survival. This is what we mean by the definition of institutional mission and role."[10] This is the work of the hour in the religious institution.

Early in this study (Chapter I) we found that historically the character of adult education changes its mission and role as the church confronts its problems and needs. This historical characteristic of the church is not unrelated to the mission and role of adult education in the contemporary church. What then is the church saying about its mission?

Those who reported on the main theme of the Second Assembly of the World Council of Churches in Evanston gave us an authoritative statement. They affirm:

> God summons the church of Jesus Christ today to speak plainly about hope. Jesus Christ is our hope. In all humility and boldness we are bound to tell the good news of the hope given to us in him.[11]

In other words, as the church faces an increasingly secular world it feels the necessity to fight the pessimism and despair of the age with a reassuring reaffirmation of hope in its gospel. Continuing on this theme the Advisory Commission stated:

> Our hope is grounded in one great Event, comprising the incarnation, ministry, death, and resurrection of Jesus Christ. . . .
>
> This tremendous Event occurred within a brief epoch which soon passed, leaving the broad scenery of history ostensibly unchanged. One concrete result alone was to be discharged: the Christian church. It appeared as a small, obscure community, unwelcomed and almost unnoticed by the great world. It knew itself to be a colony of the heavenly fatherland planted in an alien territory, and looked forward to an end lying beyond this earth and a day when the fullness of what God had done in Christ would be finally disclosed. It also knew itself to bear responsibility for the world for which Christ died, a responsibility that drove it to action and to suffering.
>
> This church still exists . . .[12]

Thus, as the church faces times of chaos and confusion it turns again to a declaration of what has traditionally been claimed the central Event in its existence. The association of the church with the Event infuses this institution with value from the Fountainhead. Institutionally speaking, it needs this infusion to offset the mounting skepticism of secular culture.

The mission of the church gained further definition at

Amsterdam as C. I. Patijin spoke the mind of the Assembly in his paper, "The Strategy of the Church."

> One fundamental issue must be made clear at the start. The church's task vis-à-vis the community in its social and political life is an indirect one. The Kingdom it proclaims is not of this world. Its task is to incorporate men in a different realm, to serve a Lord different from any the world knows. . . .
>
> It is a mistake to think that the church as an institution must adapt itself to the ways of society in order to exert its influence. It creates an impression of impotence when preachers speak more about what is in the newspaper than in the Gospels, or appeal to the same interests as those of nonchurch societies or the entertainment world. Men do not turn to the church to hear a more or less intelligent discourse on what is happening outside, but to hear its own message.[13]

Statements such as those quoted above which represent something of a consensus among authoritative voices in the councils[14] of the church can be duplicated again and again as the church discusses and reiterates its emerging theology. As the church faces a world in transition forcing a new order upon all institutions, it looks back on its origin and tradition to declare: (1) it is still God's divine institution inaugurated by his Son; (2) if there is hope for the church the hope remains in Christ; (3) it must maintain its distinctive nature regardless of pressures to be something else; and (4) the traditional roles (at least theologically speaking) remain central to the task before the church.

One does not necessarily have to agree with H. Richard Niebuhr when he states, "The results of the inquiry into the nature of the church in which theologians and churchmen are engaged today *cannot* be anticipated."[15] At least from an institutional perspective the social scientist need not be surprised at the emerging theological developments of the church in a threatening age. As far as the rationale of the church is concerned it fits the pattern of an old-line institution recasting its philosophy "without serious corruption" as a defensive reaction to a challenging age. Whether the emergent theology will be adequate for survival remains to be seen.

On the score of its own self-assessment one must acknowledge that the church has not been allowing the religious institution to drift into new areas without raising the question of purpose. One of the requirements of statesmanship in the administration of any institution is the continual sensitivity to internal and external changes and the appraisal of what these changes mean to the mission of the institution in question. We are in a time when the theological and Biblical foundations of the church have been lifted into the light of day and the church has made some decisions about what it ought to be and do.

What has been going on in the church at large has had its effect upon Christian education within the church. Paul Vieth spoke the mind of Christian educators when he stated, "Christian education has no theology which is peculiar to itself."[16] Not only have Christian educators been a part of the movement, much of what has come off the press has been from their typewriters. James Smart's *The Teaching Ministry of the Church*[17] Lewis J. Sherrill's *The Gift of Power*[18] Randolph Crump Miller's *Biblical Theology and Christian Education*[19] Howard Grimes's *The Church Redemptive*[20] and Reuel Howe's *Man's Need and God's Action*[21] could well begin such a list of contributions by educators.

Without a doubt we could go on building the case, but from what we already know about the historical pattern of education's role in reflecting the needs and problems of the church at large, the threatening characteristics of contemporary culture, and the theological patterns of response, there is little doubt about the rationale for the program of adult education in the church. *From the perspective of the theological rationale of the religious institution, the mission of adult education will undoubtedly continue a restricted pattern of concern for the nature of the religious institution and value system.* The hopes for a broad-range program of adult education under the spon-

sorship of the church do not appear bright. With so many conflicting philosophies and demands for competing institutional
support, religious institutions will have to labor hard and
long to hold their own for the minds and backs of men. Because of this abiding insecurity the church will not enjoy the
privilege of the broad delights except through an uncontrolled
drift. The range of adult education will be dictated by the
pressures upon the religious value system and the religious
institution.

EMBODIMENT OF PURPOSE

The account of the theological adjustments that the church
has been called to make as a result of the changing culture of
Western society is only one phase of institutional accommodation. Unfortunately it is all too often the only area where
discussion and concern have been focused. Although theological renaissance must come first in the order of reconstruction, the inherent weakness in the theological disciplines
has been to keep the discussions abstract and vaguely relevant
to the frustrations that prompted them in the first place. For-
tunately there is a growing awareness that discussion of the
nature and purpose of the church must be specifically related
to the embodiment of that purpose. This is where the research
of the social scientist is greatly needed by the religious institution.

Theological gap. One of the indications at the grass roots
that theological discussions have been of limited value is the
growing assent to the proposition that there is a great gap
between the theological sophistication of the scholars and the
catch-as-catch-can religion of the parishioner. Even the local
clergyman, who has lived with the scholars during his years
at seminary, quickly loses much of his theological sophistication when confronted with the professional career of building
the religious institution. Sometimes the clergyman will live a
kind of schizophrenic existence with his theological definitions of mission on one hand, his attention to day-by-day min-

isterial routine on the other, and a certain "trained in-capacity" to merge the two. More often the theological knowl-edge is simply displaced by other demands. The observations concerning the gap between the scholars and the man in the pew confirm the following statement of Randolph Crump Miller:

> There is a great gap, however, between what the Biblical schol-ars believe and teach and what the layman and church school teachers know about the Bible. This may be discovered in al-most any adult Bible class, in most preaching, and in almost all lesson materials for church schools. It is almost as if all the discoveries of more than a century are the private property of the scholars.[22]

On the other hand, when there is a consciousness of the discrepancy between the theological standards and institu-tutional demands, the pressure upon the clergyman may be difficult to resolve. One clergyman, working hard to do his best in a small church in an area where the community had marked tendencies toward the sect-type religious expression, stated confidentially and frankly:

> Sometimes it is not so much our inability to relate to the man in the pew but the fact that it would be professional suicide to make the type of approach which would build the church in such a neighborhood. . . .[23]

Another case in point is the modest acceptance of the so-called "nontheological" factors that become the warp and woof of the religious institutions but are largely ignored by the ecumenical movement.[24] The theological discussions em-body the interesting paradox of being prompted by the socio-psychological factors of contemporary society but quickly im-merse themselves in a Biblical rationale and give the ready impression of being simply and singly the acts of God. To dis-cover how quickly a "situation-conditioned"[25] theological formulation can neglect its social sources and give comparatively little attention to social and cultural factors, take in hand one of the reports of the world assemblies. There seems to be an inherent facility even among the clergy to wear one hat for theological discussions and another hat for the embodiment of institutional forms.

Administrative perversion. The first characteristic that desperately needs emphasis in a discussion of the embodiment of purpose is that "the administrative demands of the church as a social institution tend to take precedence over the sacred purposes and procedures." We have found that trends in our urban, industrial society toward the development of large-scale bureaucratic structures and the ascendency of those who manage the process of production and administration is not without parallel in the religious institution. H. Richard Niebuhr, who has done one of the best jobs of calling this phenomenon to the attention of fellow churchmen, has stated:

> It seems to be clear that the church in America in our time like the church in any place at any time is deeply influenced in its institutional forms by the political and economic society with which it lives in conjunction. As the polity of all the churches, whether they are episcopal, presbyterian, or congregational by tradition, has been modified in the direction of the political structures of Canada and the United States, so the institutional status and authority of the ministry are being modified in the direction of the democratic type of political, educational, and economic executive or managerial authority.[26]

It was also Dr. Niebuhr who coined the term "pastoral director"[27] to describe the emerging conception of the minister and to warn that inherent in it is the danger of becoming the "big operator," without reflecting the difference that Christian faith and church life require.

Likewise we recall the findings of Samuel W. Blizzard, who found that two thirds of the total ministerial workday of approximately ten hours was devoted to administration. Dr. Blizzard concluded:

> The minister is urged to spend much time organizing and administrating programs. The national church body is at the same time failing to give him an adequate theological understanding of these offices. That is the minister's dilemma.[28]

It was along this same vein that Niebuhr reported a wealth of insight as a result of his research:

> It is significant that when ministers reflect on their theological education they are likely to regret more than any other deficiency in it the failure of the school to prepare them for the administration of such a church. What these men have in mind was expressed by one of them who said in effect: The seminary prepared me for preaching and taught me the difference between preaching and public speaking; it helped me to become a pastoral counselor and not simply a counselor; it prepared me for the work of Christian education; but it gave me no preparation to administer a church as church; what I learned about church administration was a nontheological smattering of successful business practices.[29]

Thus it is not so much the fact that there are no theological definitions of what the church should be (though we shall discuss their vague and abstract qualities shortly), but that when churchmen turn to their administrative chores, little more than secular business practices evolve.

Not only does the local clergyman operate in a theological "no man's land" in respect to the embodiment of administrative duties in the local parish, but organization men of the denominational offices frequently shift into neutral when it comes to the embodiment of the theological rationale. Paul Harrison, who has done a splendid job of describing the functions of the American Baptist Convention, states:

> Each of these leaders, of course, has a personal religious faith, but as denominational officials they must maintain a theological neutrality. Officially, they are not ecclesiastical leaders but administrators of church-related agencies. An administrator is not a theologian, and religious belief must remain an adjunct to

the attainment of the goals which he has been directed to achieve. In short, there exists among the organizational men a "zone of indifference"[30] with respect to theological beliefs. They are not interested, in the first instance, in an individual's religious attitudes, but rather in his stance in relation to the work of the Convention and its agencies.[31]

Members of other denominational polities need not assume that their proverbial glass houses are made of safety glass. The obvious theological span of both the Methodist and Presbyterian churches in the nine churches of this study alone provides evidence of a range of theological embodiment and the necessity of administrative officials to hold in abeyance conflicting theological positions. As social scientists help the religious institution dig in the darkness of its own administrative catacombs they will undoubtedly reveal some theological barrenness behind the façade of each denominational polity.

Not unrelated to the current lack of theological embodiment of the nature of the church is the confusion concerning the whole concept of church as the body of Christ and the church as a secular institution. As long as the theological discussions can accent this polarity of "community" and "institution" there will be no adequate dealing with the problem of administration. Perhaps the best example of this, as Niebuhr has pointed out, is found in Prof. Emil Brunner's *The Misunderstanding of the Church*. Writes Professor Brunner: "The New Testament Ecclesia, the fellowship of Jesus Christ, is a pure communion of persons and has nothing of the character of an institution about it,"[32] and to this "Ecclesia which is always . . . a dynamic reality and nothing more, the existing churchly institutions are related as means . . . *externa subsidia*—in very diverse ways and proportions."[33]

An equally misleading barrier to the understanding and exploration of the embodiment of the theological rationale of the church is the characterization of administration as "nothing more than a way of getting things done, of accomplishing some end."[34] Such a "Christian view of administration" undercuts the whole process of examining the embodiment of purpose. It fails to acknowledge that some of the knottiest problems of administrative leadership come *after* the mission and role of the church have been defined, and *in the process* of expediting directives. It fails to realize that decision making does not terminate with definitions. It is with means that pure objectives are perverted and lack of embodiment leaves the essential nature of the church barren of any redeeming quality. The most prevalent way of perverting the mission of the church is to apply prematurely the logic of technological efficiency to the religious institution until it becomes a "smooth running machine," thus overemphasizing the neat organization and the efficient techniques of administration. Although the theological debates have served the religious institution well, the urgent demand of the hour is to examine the administrative management of the church in the light of institutional statesmanship.[35]

Even in the religious institution there are frequently decisions that so alter the original purpose that the embodiment of that purpose is never realized. As long as "the Christian view of administration" is limited to "nothing more than a way of getting things done, of accomplishing some end" the organizational men who manage local churches and denominational headquarters have within their hands immense powers to alter radically the nature of the church through the embodiment of purpose. Why should anyone concerned about the nature of the church in contemporary society not terminate the discussion with the theological definitions? Why should anyone concerned with adult education within the church look further than official statements in official documents? Why? Because theoretical definitions are never adequate descriptions!

Before we leave the consideration of administrative perversion let us further acknowledge that an overgeneralization of purpose gives free rein to a wide range of alternatives, often with the blessings of a divine mandate. If the sole directive

specified by a commander in chief to his generals in the field
is "to wage war on the enemy," it is within the range of possibility that nuclear weapons might be utilized. Unfortunately
we have many definitions of purpose within the church that
are as vague. On every hand we now hear reiterated that the
demand of the hour is for the church to "*be* the church,"
whatever that may mean. In similar fashion the Christian is
urged to accept "the Lordship of Christ." Even Professor
Niebuhr's statement without extensive elaboration is inadequate:

> When all is said and done the increase of this love of God and
> neighbor remains the purpose and the hope of our preaching
> of the gospel, of all our church organization and activity, of
> all our ministry, of all our efforts to train men for the ministry,
> of Christianity itself.[36]

The reader will recall that in Chapter II we found that the
same goal diffusion characterized the internal groups within
the church and provided little in the way of clarification for
actual objectives. As long as we continue to keep the purpose
abstract or vague we likewise allow a wide range of administrative alternatives for the embodiment of institutional character. Need we state that some of them might not be in keeping with the original design?

Struggles for integrity.   Whenever there is a loss of distinctive competence between the definition of purpose and the
embodiment of it, a comparable loss of integrity is involved.
By institutional integrity is meant "the persistence of an organization's distinctive values, competence, and role."[37] Philip
Selznick says:

> The integrity of an enterprise goes beyond efficiency, beyond
> organization forms and procedures, even beyond group cohesion.
> Integrity combines organization and policy. It is the unity that
> emerges when a particular orientation becomes so firmly a part
> of group life that it colors and directs a wide variety of atti-

tudes, decisions, and forms of organization, and does so at many levels of experience.[38]

When the purposes of an institution are vaguely or abstractly defined, when goals or values are susceptible to corruption, when fluid situations require constant adaptation, and when organizational directives are not easily imposed, an institution is especially vulnerable to loss of integrity.

Never before has the religious institution had so much competition for the affiliation and loyalty of the general population. The old New England church house, which was the center of community activities and the focal point of all that happened of importance in the village, is now an antique. The boundaries of communication and transportation that isolated these little communities from the behavior standards and values of conflicting systems have long since crumbled. For reasons such as these, indications of marginality can be identified by any who look realistically at the church in contemporary society. Values have become precarious, the authority of the professional and lay elite have been challenged, and the fragmentation of the religious institution provides little united strength. The plain fact is that the church has lost its position of prominence in the modern world, and this fact has altered its character tremendously.

One of the principal characteristics of the "new" religious institution is the other-directed recruitment obsession to gain back the prominence of yesteryear. The point of this is that manifestation of recruitment pressures upon the church pervert the embodiment of purpose defined so vigorously in the current theological self-assessment. Evangelism now becomes mainly the "Book of Numbers." Preaching tends to relinquish its prophetic functions and turns to more and more salesmanship. Social education and action programs play it safe so that there is no alienation of tenuously held affiliates. Worship has a theater-type orientation and is dependent upon professionals. Church architecture also tends to reflect the showmanship of the church rather than provide for the distinctive functions of the religious community and proclaim this distinctiveness. And so the story of the perversion of the high aspirations continues and the integrity of the religious complex is strained.

The infusion of value that is needed on every hand in the church is not necessarily that which helps the individual become Christian but that which has an institutional purpose foremost. The personal satisfactions that bring the affiliates to the church week after week are not alone the religious experiences, but frequently the purely recreational. The koinonia implies more than a mere human association, but the contemporary church would be hard pressed to maintain its present institution if it had to rely upon the fellowship of the Spirit alone. Furthermore, the local church cannot maintain itself as an institution unless it recruits a sizable nucleus of workers to care for its program. At this point the distinctive goals of the Kingdom of God and institution-building become blurred and the lack of clarification further frustrates the struggle for integrity.

In brief, then, the religious institution is particularly vulnerable to lack of integrity in the embodiment of institutional purpose. The religious institution can adopt many of the efficient methods of the business world, but integrity must go beyond efficiency; the religious institution may define its theology and polity with an air of pride in its theoretical accomplishments, but integrity is more than theoretical formulations; the religious institution may even develop a group cohesion and camaraderie, but integrity goes even beyond this. "Integrity is the unity that emerges when a particular orientation becomes so firmly a part of group life that it colors and directs a wide variety of attitudes, decisions, and forms of organization, and does so at many levels of experience." The religious institution with its catch-as-catch-can affiliates, its low-level participation, its proliferation of internal groups, and the overwhelming force of external conflicting values and norms of behavior forcibly confronting religious affiliates finds it extremely difficult to maintain a thoroughgoing integrity.

Incentives and insecurity. There is probably no place where the perversion of institutional integrity takes place more vividly than in the area of incentives. In Chapter V we documented the value infusion necessary for recruitment, sustaining interest, deployment of personnel, financial support, and for internal stratification. When such basic organizational needs are so difficult to satisfy, it is not surprising that the message of the institution becomes warped here and there to support these needs, or it may be lost in default because there is little time for its emphasis. Nor is it surprising that the religious institution builds upon other supporting values that come from nonreligious personal satisfactions in social situations. Although such characteristics may be easy for the outsider to see, they may be difficult for the committed churchman to identify. His personal involvement in these characteristics make them all appear natural and commonplace in the routine of his daily tasks.

If the nature of society were otherwise, it might be possible for the church to embody the "remnant" concept of Old Testament times in which relatively few people developed an organization in depth rather than an all-inclusive veneer with a highly secular character. The plain fact is that the remnant is not a common characteristic of any significant portion of the church. The church does not go deep and apply its purpose without corruption in the concrete acts of embodying the high resolves of its theologically defined purpose. The church is rarely restrictive with standards and demands. Instead, the church has adopted the standards of success of secular society, where large numbers signify power, authority, and status for the church.

In brief, the theological and ethical authority of the church has not carried through. The church in contemporary society has represented an extreme form of adaptive organization that has drifted into behavior patterns like those of secular institutions. This was well illustrated recently when one church held a congregational meeting under the banner of "First Church Unlimited." This banner was followed by another twenty-five-foot sign that read, "The first requirement of successful salesmanship is knowledge." The purpose of the meeting was to generate enthusiasm about the church and its future and to send a newly organized "flock" out to sell members and friends on the church and its distinctive attributes.

As goes the corruption of institutional integrity in the church so goes the character of adult education. The educational program of the church is a child of its parent body and takes its character from it. The ministers and directors of Christian education are staff personnel dependent upon the clergy for policy and program direction. On the other hand, they are required to develop a phase of church life that enjoys little institutional support. Possessing low status among their colleagues their professional success is contingent upon their personal success in developing a quality educational program amid the pronounced institutional limitations we have identified. Is there any wonder that the turnover in this special ministry is so high? It takes unusual dedication for capable personnel to persist.

Patterns of internal tension. The social scientist has not been surprised at the rational development of the religious organization. He has learned to expect that, as social organizations develop into larger and more formal organizational structures, a division of labor appears with specialization as guiding principle and delegation as a common phenomenon, and that a hierarchy of authority evolves with mechanisms of co-ordination and channels of communication to bring vital information to responsible officials. These have been common phenomena to large-scale organizations in industrial society. Although the churchmen have not had the same sophisticated understanding of what has taken place, they have observed and griped about the "red tape," the "pressures of headquarters," the "politics," and more recently the "institutionalism" of the church. But let us not assume that it has always been a disappointing observation for churchmen. In the first place the religious institution has profited on many occasions by the adoption of bureaucratic mechanisms. In the second place a legitimacy for it was found in Scripture: had it not been ordained that "some should be apostles, and prophets, some evangelists, some pastors and teachers, for the equipment of the saints, for the work of the ministry"?[39]

On the other hand, not all of the developments have been that easily accommodated. There has been an emerging feeling that when the religious institution rationalizes its organizational structures it becomes something else than the "holy" community and the very nature of the church has been altered. Furthermore, there has been a growing sensitivity to the fact that individuals have not found spiritually satisfying experiences in the roles that make up the rationally administered religious institution.[40] Even more interesting for our purposes is the fact that the religious educator has been among the more disturbed voices of the religious functionaries. Could it be that the insecurities of the educator's role prompts these concerns? The chasm that exists between the theologically defined redemptive community and the sociologically defined religious institution is nowhere more apparent than in the educational work of the church. Here, too, the integrity of the religious community has been put under stress.

The voices of Christian educators in the church have become more and more pointed concerning what the teaching function of the church *ought* to be. Dr. Smart has emphatically stated the mind of the Christian educator when he opens his book, *The Teaching Ministry of the Church,* with the blast:

> The existence of Christian education as a distinct area of study and action in the church rests upon the assumption that the church of Jesus Christ has, of necessity, a teaching function. The church must teach, just as it must preach, or it will not be the church. Responsibility for teaching rests upon the whole church even though only certain members undertake specific teaching assignments. . . . Teaching belongs to the essence of

the church and a church that neglects this function of teaching
has lost something that is indispensable to its nature as a
church. . . .

Strange as it may seem, this foundation principle of Christian education remains largely unrecognized today, and, strang-
est of all, unrecognized often by those who are devoting their
lives to the work of teaching in the church.[41]

A chapter in another book that serves well in feeling the
pulse of the Christian educator is that of David H. Ernsberger,
entitled "The Centrality of Adult Education." Among other
strong statements Ernsberger declares:

Although the theologians of the Reformation did not use the
term "adult education" as such, it is clear that they regarded
the educating of adults as central to the purpose of the ministry. . . .

The recovery of the doctrine of the ministry that emerged
from the Reformation would first result in upsetting present
ministerial preferences and valuations concerning the relative
importance of teaching. Instead of being regarded as *least* important and instead of receiving the *smallest* proportion of the
minister's time, which Blizzard's survey indicates is the prevailing
tendency today, the teaching role would be placed at the top
of the list, alongside the preaching role. The present hierarchy
of ministerial preferences, with preaching at the top and teaching at the bottom, would become simply untenable for anyone
who came to espouse Protestantism's traditional theological conception of the ministry.[42]

Thus, one of the marked characteristics in the internal tension of the educational role of the church is dissatisfaction
with the embodiment of education in the nature and purpose
of the church. As stated above, the educators have been responsible for many of the books concerning the nature of the
church and the character of the religious experience. Without
a doubt theological foundations are being discussed today
among the church's educators as never before. Could it be that

this is prompted only by the inadequate embodiment of educational functions in the characteristics of the religious institution? Might it not also be prompted by the continual frustrations of building educational program where such institutional support is weak? Let us look at the direction this discussion has taken in recent years for its sociological significance.

Internal tension is observable in the distinction between preaching *and* teaching in the views of C. H. Dodd on *kērygma* and *didachē* (preaching and teaching in the New Testament) which has had widespread acceptance. Declared Dodd: "The New Testament writers draw a clear distinction between preaching and teaching. The distinction is preserved alike in Gospels, Acts, Epistles, and Apocalypse."[43] Perhaps the reason for this widespread acceptance was the fact that the preaching and teaching roles within the ministry were themselves taking on distinctive characteristics and the theoretical explanation fit the functional fact. It provided the theoretical legitimacy for what in fact already existed.

More recently the widespread acceptance of Dodd's dichotomy has come in for some sharp criticism. The feeling has been voiced that the polarity has been too sharply drawn and that the educational work of the church has been associated with insipid moralism while the preaching function held on to what was fundamental to the church. The resultant harm of this ideology for the educational work of the church has been felt. The distinction, however, has been retained even by some of Dodd's critics, though the unity and necessity of both have been accented. Explains one critic:

> We must try to see why this ministry of the word is twofold. Why must there be preaching *and* teaching? Why is not one sufficient? The fact of the difference between the two is evident wherever we look. In the Old Testament, what the prophet does as a preacher of the word is something different from what he or any other adult in Israel does as teacher, yet not so different as to destroy the unity between the two. In the New Testament,

one word is not sufficient to describe either the ministry of Jesus or the ministry of the apostles. They are both preachers and teachers. So also in the present-day church. Preaching is preaching and teaching is teaching, and yet good preaching is also teaching and good teaching has in it the note of the preacher's proclamation. Wherein are they together, and wherein are they different?

They are together in being both the service of the Word of God. . . . Preaching essentially is the proclamation of this Word of God *to man in his unbelief.* . . .

Teaching essentially (but not exclusively) addresses itself to the situation of the man who has repented and turned to God and to the situation of children of believers who through the influence of their parents have in them a measure of faith, even though they have also in them a large measure of unbelief.[44]

The crucial point in this latter view is the emphasis that *both are essential to a full ministry.* Neither preaching nor teaching outranks the other. No status is lost for the teaching role of the church in this rationale.

Another view frequently voiced is that the educational work of the church has complete unity with that of the church as a whole. This is what Howard Grimes means when he states that there is

. . . no real dichotomy between nurture and evangelism, no absolute division between *kērygma* and *didachē,* no neat packaging of the offices of the Christian community.[45]

It has also been stated succinctly by Paul Vieth:

Today the emphasis is on the unity of the whole church program, including Christian education. As the church has one Lord, so it has one faith and one ministry. That ministry is expressed by varied gifts through different offices. It is not possible to draw sharp lines of distinction between the different functions of the church. Christian education may take place at almost any point in the church's program, even though there is a segment of that program (the church school) whose primary concern is Christian education.[46]

Here again the educational function of the church does not lose status in the eyes of the educator, because there is no phase of the life of the church where in some measure the educational experience is alien to the highest experience of God. In brief, the educational experience cannot be divorced from the church in its essence.

Even more bold than the view that equates the educational function and role of the church with the preaching role is the occasional declaration, more and more frequent among educators, in which the supremacy of the educational function is declared. Ernsberger makes such a statement when he writes:

> A doctrine of the ministry that stresses the teaching role above all, and that nevertheless is able to relate all other ministerial roles to the teaching role in a way that clarifies their significance, provides the minister with a core of professional integrity and coherence in the light of which all his various functions may be seen and evaluated.[47]

Although such statements are not found readily in print, conversations with Christian educators frequently accent the primacy of the educator's role in accomplishing the true work of the church. Small groups in particular have been given credit for establishing a more meaningful relationship between man and God than a host of preaching services.

It is not the writer's purpose to discuss the validity of the educators' claims but to report the emphasis they give to their role. However, it is significant that the educator loses no status in enhancing the educational role of the church. Such a rationale places the educator in a more favorable position among his colleagues theoretically if not functionally.

In the light of the observable subordinate indices characterizing the educational work of the church such declarations of religious educators are not surprising. The educators have felt the insecurity of their roles and the low status of their work at every point. There is a dichotomy between preaching and teaching, but its most pronounced manifestations are not in the area of the theoretical rationale but in the area of the functional embodiment of theory. As the organizational structure of the religious institution tended to be patterned after the bureaucratically oriented secular structures, as the educator came to be more and more a staff specialist, as the educational enterprise of the church tended toward marginality, and as the religious values became more and more precarious, the resulting insecurities of the Christian educator have called for a reappraisal of the nature and purpose of the church. If there are any equalities in the functions and roles of the religious enterprise, they are of a kingdom not of this world—a "holy" community. In the meantime the Christian educator must live much of life in a subordinate role of tension and frustration. A pathology of fictions between the two worlds makes it possible for the discrepancy to be lived with.

Patterns of differentiation. In spite of the reduction of social differences of race, class sectionalism, and nationalism, and the signs of growing cultural unity through mass communication, common values, styles of life, etc., which have recently been documented as social sources of church unity, it has been the observation of this researcher that there are still ample means of differentiation in the religious enterprise.[48] In fact, the material in Chapter III and elsewhere prompts the question of whether there ever is a social group divested of means of social differentiation by which it imprints its image upon the patterns of internal structure and order. We may in all accuracy report the reduction of certain traditional patterns of social differentiation, but does the social group not "invent" other distinctions to take their places, or further refine what seems to have been blurred? Such a question needs further research as we come to the close of this study.

Prominent illustrations are to be found in the three downtown churches on which we have focused. Progressive deterioration, changing racial constituency, constant mobility, and a wide range of socioeconomic and cultural variables between the immediate neighborhood and neighborhoods of the present membership, provide so many bases for social differentiation that frustrations in social integration remain the "kiss of death" for more churches in our inner cities than we care to think about. There may be a "common-core Protestantism" emerging, but there are also frustrations of differentiation so powerful as to threaten the very existence of the downtown church.

Furthermore, as we probe into the matter of social differentiation we find that an intricate array of sociological phenomena serves as a screening process. A wide range of differentiating factors and variables acts to give the local church a distinctive social base and a distinctive "personality." Before reaching the church school class or the adult group the participant has been exposed to a multitude of differentiating experiences upon which he and others have made some overt or covert judgment. The participant does not simply open a door and walk into a class convened for the discussion of some announced subject. He becomes a functioning part of a complex social milieu.

As we observe the path of the participant and the place of the educational group within the church we further observe that the institution dominates the educational cell within the parent body. Hence, what we find in observing the selective social base supports what we have found elsewhere in this study, namely, that the educational group within the church is destined to play a complementary but subordinate role within the institution. It will not merely serve the ends of the parent institution, but its social composition will be colored by its peculiar social characteristics.

Let us not forget that this screening process would not exist if it were not for the fact that the participant is a free agent. If the institution had the leverage of law as in the case of public education or the financial incentives of business and industry, there would be more leverage and control of the participant, and undoubtedly more tolerance of differentiating factors by the participant. As it is, the participant can easily change his religious affiliation or simply not attend the educational or other functions of the religious institution. Therefore, we can expect a rather low-pressure climate for adult education in the church.

Furthermore, a homogeneous social composition for an educational group raises numerous questions concerning the character of the experience. How much range of experience do the participants bring to the discussions? How does social homogeneity influence the control of the group and the teaching methodology utilized? How does social selectivity influence the range of program sponsorship by the religious institution? What action patterns are typical as a result of such an education setting? These and similar questions must wait for further research but prompt some interesting speculation.

Marginal insecurities. Although the church in America has been successfully adding numbers of people to its membership roles and has enjoyed an increased interest in religion, most observers have agreed that when the façade has been washed away, the degree of involvement in the message and mission of the church is slight indeed. The church, which was once the dominant institution in the community, has been supplanted by numerous social collectives that have massed equal if not superior power to influence society. As the church has been pushed to the periphery of community life, low status, little power, and insecurity have resulted.

One of the characteristics of marginality as a prime source of insecurity in institutions is the tendency to adapt the institution to existing pressures and make accommodations to acquire strength. It undercuts institutional leadership by draining from it the autonomy necessary for decision making. This, of course, introduces the problem of institutional integrity, for the question which now rears its ugly head is "How much can an institution adapt and still remain true to its essential mission?" The Messinger account of the Townsend Movement and the Gusfield report of the W.C.T.U. discussed above provide two concrete examples of organizations faced with this dilemma. The dilemma of adaptation is not a problem unknown to the religious institution.

The theological reassessment which has been discussed above has been prompted in large measure by the problem of adaptation in the face of marginal insecurity. By affirming "traditional" theological positions, our theological leaders have said, in effect, that the religious institution has gone too far in its accommodation of existing culture. On the other hand, we can easily notice a proliferation of programs that come close to pure recreation. This seeming paradox is made possible by the existence of the theological gap, the dichotomy between aspiration and actuality and the fictions that make for institutional pathology. As long as the great divorce can be perpetuated, institutional leadership can live with the situation. But just this long, the integrity of the institution will not bear the scrutiny of the careful observer. Adult educators are most frequently identified with this dilemma because of their responsibility for the group life of the church and the character of group programs.

Adult educators are also affected by the fact that the type of activities an institution will engage in to win, maintain, and utilize affiliates as agents forces its character upon the program of adult education. This is due to a second major finding that more pronounced marginality characterizes the educational work within the religious institution. Because of this the educational program of the church can be expected to be subservient to the institution's general objectives, expend a great deal of energy in a value infusion of the institutional perspective, and swim against an undertow of institutional salesmanship.

These are but a few of the effects of marginal insecurity that have been given space in this report, but they do not exhaust the list. Burton Clark also indicated some of the pervasive effects of marginal insecurity when he wrote:

This status affects almost everything the organization does, for no single attribute of organization colors thought and action more than a deep-seated insecurity. It affects employee morale, the incentives offered in recruitment of new employees, the feasibility of making long-range plans, the stability of budget, relationships with other departments, and the level of organization at which decisions are made.[49]

Beyond the definition of mission and role lies the task of building purpose into the religious institution so that these definitions develop depth and bear fruit. The religious institution is now faced with the fact that great attenuation and distortion characterizes the religious enterprise and the educational program and personnel are right in the heart of it. It is hoped that the reader will now appreciate more fully that there is *no sharp division between tasks of defining mission and embodying purpose, and that many pathological conditions jeopardize the mission of adult education in the church.*

MISSION IN JEOPARDY

It is hoped that the reader of these pages has gained an appreciation of administration as a thoroughgoing, day-by-day activity and not merely the occasional policy meetings of an "official board" or even the technical engineering of getting a job done. Both these aspects of administration are important to the life of the church and both policy making and attending to the narrow practical aims are common experiences for the church. What is not well understood is what happens between the policy making and the expediting of administrative objectives that alter the whole character of the institution. It has been the intention here to fill in some of the blanks that affect the program of adult education in the church.

Furthermore it is hoped that the reader will gain an appreciation for the fact that the description of the mission of an institution, or of any phase of its existence, is more than a theoretical statement of purpose. Likewise the mission of education in the church cannot be described by statements that declare it the "indispensable human channel through which God's grace and truth may reach all men," or that "Christian education for adults is an indispensable corollary of the gospel." When we look at the actual embodiment of such purpose we find that the mission of adult education has been perverted by an intricate complex of factors that undermine the institution's high aspirations.

Such statements of purpose then become fictions or myths. For those individuals unable to identify or face the functional discrepancies, the myth becomes a successful mechanism of bridging the chasm between aspiration and actuality. This is especially true for those professional educators whose career demands that they live with these frustrations day by day. Such professionals actually become the most vociferous proponents of the "educational myth." Since they have responsibility for the educational program of the church such myths serve in the satisfaction of their daily responsibilities.

This, however, should not be construed to mean that professional educators in the church consciously utilize fictions as a means to accomplish their responsibilities, even though this may occasionally be the case. Although the centrality of the educational work of the church may be a fiction for the total system, it is not necessarily the case for the educator. In fact, the educator may adopt, internalize, and honestly work on the assumption of the central importance of the educational role for the church. Such an educator finds a personal, internal integrity which is not characteristic of the religious institution as a whole.

Yet, at the same time the sharp discrepancies between theory and practice are taking their toll in the church. Not only is the educational mission of the church unrealized, but numerous so-called practical problems are not finding solution, and the character of the institution as well as the program of adult education is being affected.

These observations have been made by one who believes

that the Christian orientation is indispensable for the reconstruction of individuals and institutions in an age of crisis and change. Never before has the world needed the "development of mature, wise, and responsible citizens who can participate intelligently in a free society."[50] The Christian message contributes immeasurably to such development when its gospel is realized in good measure.

Furthermore, the religious institution in America has attracted greater numbers of adults since World War II than in any other era in American history. Although the church has undoubtedly played a more significant role in community life in bygone years, it can still accumulate impressive statistics of those who have some affiliation, if only tangential. In brief, the church not only has a redemptive and responsible gospel but a point of contact. Here is a tremendous potential for creative encounter.

Yet much current Christian expression reflects the color of the social institution and is directed toward its distinctive problems and needs, rather than to a broad range of human problems. The needs of the church to secure itself in a threatening age have caused the church to turn its gospel toward securing the religious institution rather than serving the society at large. The full gospel has been limited to those aspects which serve to enhance the religious institution, often doing damage to the central message by its perversion. The question of the hour is: To what degree can adult education in the American religious institution become a redemptive medium in contemporary culture in the "development of mature, wise, and responsible citizens who can participate (with their gospel) intelligently," with institutional insecurities being what they are? If the religious institution has such difficulty embodying its purpose independent of its pressures for self-preservation, can its program of adult education be responsible?

SUMMARY OF FINDINGS

1. The church has been described here as an old-line institution, with adult education playing a significant role in the institution from the very beginning. Through a process of institutionalization, built-in rigidities mediate against rapid adaptation and accommodation. Therefore, one would not expect the program of adult education in the church to adapt easily to new pressures.

2. Social and psychological changes in society, taking place at an increasingly rapid rate, are to be numbered among the "real" causes of schism that have divided the religious establishment into many different organizational structures and substructures. As a consequence one can expect that adult education would vary somewhat according to the distinctive clientele of a particular religious institution.

3. As institutional needs and problems of the church changed, the types of adult education also changed to meet these varying needs. This characteristic suggests that adult education under the sponsorship of the church gains its directives from sources other than the purely educational and that education is in a subservient and marginal relationship to other interests.

4. The church itself is in a marginal position in American

society. The church in America is no match for the large social collectives because it has spawned a proliferation of separate religious organizations that fragment the total religious enterprise. Although the ecumenical movement has tended to direct some energies toward unity, the great bulk of the religious effort is turned inward toward the sustaining of individual local churches and individual denominations. As a consequence, adult education must concern itself with selling and defending the religious enterprise and the denominational institutions in an increasingly secular and disinterested culture.

5. A position of dependency, which characterized the relationship of the educational operation within the parent institution, has been a persistent historical phenomenon.

6. The diffuseness of educational goals makes it possible for educational activities to be directed at will to focus attention on the distinctive institutional needs and problems of the hour.

7. The adult group participants come into their associations screened through an intricate array of sociological phenomena that serve to provide a relatively homogeneous social base for the educational process. These participants bring a certain external set of sentiments, activities, and patterns of interaction which need further research, since they suggest numerous limiting characteristics of the range of referents and resources.

8. Other institutional satisfactions dominate activities of adult education in the church to the extent that unless the experiences in the sanctuary are satisfactory, there will be little if any follow-through in classrooms. This indicates that the major portion of the recruitment for educational groups was predicated on previous satisfactions with the cultic characteristics of the "front room."

9. The religious institution has a very tenuous hold upon the participants in its adult groups. The participants in the religious institutions are in a "buyer's market" with an array

of religious experiences to select from and a freedom to transfer affiliation at will. Educational program must constantly be weighed against the possible alienation of church members and/or the winning of new members. This has made for a rather low-pressure educational program on the part of both the participants and the teaching personnel.

10. The tendency toward informal organization and the primary relations in the small groups with which the local church abounds accents the process of differentiation in the more intimate personal relations and serves to narrowly stratify the adult group participants.

11. Since interdenominational agencies are dependent upon denominational structures for leadership and support, adult education under their sponsorship is subject to the same marginality that characterizes the denominations. Because they draw their support from the denominations instead of having access to an independent base from which to speak authoritatively, adult education under interdenominational sponsorship must reflect the marginality of the religious institution as a whole.

12. When interdenominational bodies sponsor adult education, it is usually considered peripheral rather than central to the work of the church. Because of the dependency of the interdenominational bodies, adult education under their sponsorship must not compete with, but must be supplementary to, denominational and local church activities.

13. The future development of adult education under the sponsorship of interdenominational bodies will continue much the same as in the past except for the possibility of picking up new services that meet the need of the church—services that the denominational bodies have not developed.

14. Adult education under the sponsorship of interdenominational bodies is hampered by fragmentation resulting from numerous, un-co-ordinated small units which drastically limit the resources available to develop new programs. Serious limitations were evident in the lack of full-time staff members in

state or local councils charged with responsibilities for adult education.

15. That councils of churches have no corner on inter-denominational adult education was evident in the Bay Area with the development of the Laymen's School of Religion, which chose to orbit around the seminaries instead of the councils. With this change in sponsorship came a more free, independent, and critical type of adult education, although its future at this writing is still somewhat precarious.

16. The traditional explanations of denominational polity are not satisfactory for any realistic characterization of de-nominational organizations because a blurring of theoretical distinctions has come about mainly through the adoption of bureaucratic characteristics common to all large-scale organizations in modern society. As a result the religious institution has provided clear-cut divisions of labor in which specialists are hired on the basis of technical qualifications, a stratified hierarchy of authority, standardized procedures and "products," and impersonality in dealing with large numbers of people. Although there have been some significant resistances to check the rapid swing of the religious institution into the orbit of the rational pursuit of efficiency through bureaucratic procedures, there have been some major strides in this direction. In this process adult education came to be considered a specialty function and educators are seen as staff specialists who implement the educational program at the dictate of administrators who manage the religious enterprise. Adult education gains access to its public only through adopting and aiding the general goals and objectives of the line officers, who in turn reflect the current needs and problems of the organization.

17. Because the local church has such a tenuous hold upon the rank-and-file membership it is a weak link in the rational pursuit of efficiency via the bureaucratization of the religious institution. The inability of the local unit to rationally administrate its affairs limits the restriction of educational

program to that which is designated solely for institutional security. Observations in this study indicate that occasionally adult groups drifted into other types of educational activity and frequently into purely social interests.

18. Occasionally the recruitment needs of the local church have served as the motivation of program of adult education. In some cases the type of adult education makes a religious institution more attractive in the eyes of certain publics. For example, forums on pertinent local, national, and international affairs mark the church as "progressive" or "liberal" and hence more attractive in the eyes of certain publics.

19. Adult education has its best chance for development in large churches with multiple staffs. Because of the unusually large expenditure of energy which the local clergyman invests in the administration of the local church the potential for adult education increases as the size of the staff increases.

20. The ideological brotherhood between religion and education embodying concerns about the "cultural" characteristics of the "good life" have not only bucked the trend toward the bureaucratization of the religious institution but have also provided some status to religious structures with the educational objectives. However, the checking of bureaucratic developments has also stunted adult education that might have developed through the increased resources of a more rationally administered institution.

21. The insecurities of the local church as a distinctive type of unit in the denominational organization tend to restrict the development of a broad range of educational enterprises in favor of those activities which help secure the local church as an organization.

22. The infusion of value which naturally results as a reaction to institutional insecurities tends to characterize adult education in the church by emphases upon the distinctive competence of the religious institution, the distinctive qualities of the religious life, the distinctive character of the religious ideology, and the distinctive values of religious leader-

ship. This distinctive type of education, prompted by the needs and problems of the religious institution, is more highly prized than education for the sake of knowledge itself.

23. The concern for recruitment tends to socialize a priority of behavior patterns of the sanctuary as superior to those of the classroom. The massification, spectator, theater-type trend in contemporary religious institutions is not conducive to the requirements of an adequate educational program by any measure.

24. The "irrationality" of the local church places significant limitations upon the organization and administration of a broadly ranged program of adult education under the sponsorship of the church. With limitations of communication, authority, and control inherent in the local situation considerable energy is directed to these necessities before the other educational "embellishments" can be considered.

25. The weaknesses in the formal support of the local clergyman and the consequent dependence upon administration through informal mechanisms require such an energy expenditure that the local clergyman ventures to add little to his administrative load through the addition of extra program. With such a drain upon clerical leadership there is limited opportunity for additional educational program to be inaugurated.

26. The stratification system of the local church mediates against the development of educational program. This system relegates the professional educator to the role of specialist working in one of the tributaries (not the main stream) of the life of the church; and his salary, office and equipment, budget, position in the communication channels, etc., are indices of this. Likewise the educator must build his program among the laity in a stratification system that provides little support for program development. Teachers are "low men on the totem pole" in comparison with other leadership roles. Yet the expenditure of energy required for the role is considerable.

27. The building of program for adult education in the local church meets further resistances in the conservative nature of the religious institution. The management of existing programs is much easier to accomplish than bucking the conservative nature of established habits, values, vested interests, and other rigidities characteristic of all old-line institutions.

28. An active discussion of the nature of the church has been providing the religious institution with the top-level definition of the mission and role that is necessary to any surviving institution in times of rapid social change. It has been the theologian more than any other religious leader to whom the church has looked to "specify and recast the general aims of the church so as to adapt them without serious corruption, to the requirements of institutional survival." In the main the theological discussions have reaffirmed the traditional declarations with a resulting "new" orthodoxy. Curriculum materials and leadership training conferences have reflected this theological activity with attempts to curtail the "frills" of group activity and introduce a divine constraint upon the Christian education of adults.

29. It should not go without notice that the Christian educators have been active in the reassessment of the religious institution and have written the educational process into the very center of the nature of the church. Although this should be recognized as a sincere attempt to infuse the low status educational role with theological respectability and greater appreciation, it is also evident that the character of the educational enterprise will support the divine constraint rather than the "rambling delights" wherever clerical leadership can speak authoritatively.

NOTES

Introduction

1. *Christian Education in Our Church* (Board of Christian Education of the United Presbyterian Church in the U.S.A., revised October, 1959), p. 7. Italics supplied.

2. Bernard E. Meland, *The Church and Adult Education* (American Association for Adult Education, 1939), p. 1.

3. C. Ellis Nelson, "The Divine Constraint of Christian Education for Adults," *Westminster Adult Leader*, curriculum periodical of The United Presbyterian Church in the U.S.A. Vol. 2, No. 1 (October–December, 1958), pp. 3–4. Previously printed in the *Union Seminary Quarterly Review* (November, 1957).

4. For one-volume texts in the sociology of religion, cf. Michael Argyle, *Religious Behavior* (The Free Press of Glencoe, 1959); Thomas Ford Hoult, *The Sociology of Religion* (Holt, Rinehart & Winston, Inc., 1958); Elizabeth K. Nottingham, *Religion and Society* (Random House, Inc., 1954); Joachim Wach, *Sociology of Religion* (University of Chicago Press, 1944); and J. Milton Yinger, *Religion, Society and the Individual* (The Macmillan Company, 1957).

5. The author is particularly indebted to the theoretical system as developed by Philip Selznick. See *Leadership in Administration: A Sociological Interpretation* (Row, Peterson & Company, 1957).

6. Burton Clark, *Adult Education in Transition: A Study of Institutional Insecurity* (University of California Press, 1958).

7. *Ibid.*, p. 154.

Chapter I. The Background of Adult Education in the Church

1. Lewis Joseph Sherrill, *The Rise of Christian Education* (The Macmillan Company, 1953), p. 86.

2. Ernst Troeltsch, *The Social Teaching of the Christian Churches,* Vol. I, tr. by Olive Wyon (The Macmillan Company, 1931), p. 39.

3. Institutionalization has been defined as "the development of orderly, stable, socially intergrating forms and structures out of unstable, loosely patterned, or merely technical types of action." Leonard Broom and Philip Selznick, *Sociology: A Text with Adapted Readings* (Row, Peterson & Company, 1953), p. 238.

4. Sherrill, *op. cit.,* pp. 144–153.

5. *Ibid.,* pp. 160–163.

6. Max Weber, who introduced the term "charisma" into the language of the sociologist, also differentiated between *personal* charisma, which is due to personal qualifications, and the charisma of *office.* The transfer of charisma from the original personal character of the leader to the office of the leader is a common phenomenon in institutionalization. For a good discussion of charisma and leadership, see Joachim Wach, *Sociology of Religion* (University of Chicago Press, 1944), pp. 337–341.

7. Kenneth Scott Latourette, *A History of Christianity* (Harper & Brothers, 1953), p. 81.

8. Sherrill, *op. cit.,* p. 186.

9. *Ibid.,* pp. 186–187.

10. *Ibid.,* p. 188.

11. For an excellent survey of religious dissent and ecumenical efforts, see Ruth Rouse and Stephen Charles Neill, eds., *A History of the Ecumenical Movement* (The Westminster Press, 1954).

12. *Ibid.,* p. 20. See also Latourette, *op. cit.,* pp. 447–458.

13. Benson Y. Landis, ed., *Yearbook of American Churches,* 1959 (National Council of the Churches of Christ in the U.S.A., p. 252.

14. Rouse and Neill, *op. cit.,* p. 221.

15. H. Richard Niebuhr, *The Social Sources of Denominationalism* (Henry Holt & Company, Inc., 1929), pp. 19–20.

16. Troeltsch, *op. cit.,* pp. 331–336.

17. H. Richard Niebuhr, *The Social Sources of Denominationalism,* pp. 19–20.

18. Liston Pope, *Millhands and Preachers: A Study of Gastonia* (Yale University Press, 1948), pp. 122–124.

19. Robert Lee, *The Social Sources of Church Unity* (Abington Press, 1960), pp. 21–74.

20. Martin E. Marty, *The New Shape of American Religion* (Harper & Brothers, 1958), p. 2.

21. Will Herberg, *Protestant—Catholic—Jew: An Essay in American Religious Sociology* (Alfred A. Knopf, Inc., 1951), pp. 304–342.

22. Yinger, *op. cit.,* p. 280.

23. Robin Williams, *American Society* (Alfred A. Knopf, Inc., 1951), pp. 304–342.

24. Elmer T. Clark, "Nontheological Factors in Religious Diversity," *The Ecumenical Review,* Vol. III (July, 1951), p. 355. For a further elaboration of the theme that more than doctrine divides the churches, see also Walter G. Muelder, "Institutionalism in Relation to Unity and Dis-

unity," *The Nature of the Unity We Seek,* Paul S. Minear, ed. (The Bethany Press, 1958), pp. 90–102, and Muelder's other paper "Institutional Factors Affecting Unity and Disunity," *The Ecumenical Review,* Vol. VIII (January, 1956), pp. 113–126.

25. William James, *The Varieties of Religious Experience* (originally published by Longmans, Green & Co., 1902).

26. Troeltsch, *op. cit.*

27. Emile Durkheim, *The Elementary Forms of Religious Life,* tr. by Joseph W. Swain (George Allen & Unwin, Ltd., London, 1915. Reprinted by The Free Press of Glencoe, 1947).

28. H. Richard Niebuhr, *The Social Sources of Denominationalism.*

29. For example, following a letter by C. H. Dodd to *The Ecumenical Review* there have been a series of papers published in successive issues on the nontheological aspects of the ecumenical movement. See C. H. Dodd, "A Letter Concerning Unavowed Motives in Ecumenical Discussions," *The Ecumenical Review,* Vol. II (Autumn, 1949), pp. 52–56; Jacques Ellul, "On the Cultural and Social Factors Influencing Church Division," *The Ecumenical Review,* Vol. IV (April, 1952), pp. 269–275; G. R. Cragg, "Disunities Created by Differing Patterns of Church Life," *The Ecumenical Review,* Vol. IV (April, 1952), pp. 276–281.

30. S. L. Greenslade, *Schism in the Early Church* (Harper & Brothers, 1953), pp. 37–124.

31. Yinger, *op. cit.,* p. 138.

32. *Ibid.*

33. Burton Clark, *op. cit.*

Chapter II. Marginality and the Religious Institution

1. For a good survey of the indices of this contemporary religious "enthusiasm," see Herberg, *op. cit.,* Ch. IV.

2. "Who Belongs to What Church?", *The Catholic Digest* (January, 1953). This research which was conducted by Ben Gaffin and Associates reported that church preference for adults over 18 indicated that 95 per cent (68 per cent Protestants, 23 per cent Catholics, 4 per cent Jews) indicated their religious identification. Only 5 per cent indicated no preference.

Information Service (National Council of Churches) (January 21, 1950). This survey of churches in twenty-three metropolitan districts, made by the committee for Co-operative Field Research indicated that "in none of them did more than 7 per cent of the people fail to give themselves a religious classification."

Public Opinion News Service (March 20, 1955). In the results of this Gallup Poll made in early 1955, 96.9 per cent were found to identify themselves religiously (70.8 per cent Protestants, 22.9 per cent Catholics, 3.1 per cent Jews) and 3.1 per cent gave answers that placed them in the "other," "none" categories.

3. Landis, *op. cit.* Although there is notorious confusion in religious statistics, this yearbook places the figure at 109,557,741. See also "The Year the Revival Passed," *The Christian Century.* Vol. LXXV (December 31,

1958), pp. 1490–1501. This editorial stated: "The revival in its present form is ending, it seems to us, for three reasons. First, the original energies are dissipating; second, the American public is tiring; third, opposition is reappearing among the 'cultured despisers.'"

4. New church construction rose from 49 millions in 1939 to 768 millions in 1956. For the annual increase of church building during these years, see U.S. Department of Commerce, *Construction Volume and Costs* (statistical supplement to *Construction Review*, Vol. III, 1957), pp. 14–25.

5. Herberg, *op. cit.*, p. 60.

6. See Fletcher Coates, "Is the Religious Revival in the U.S. Real?" *National Council Outlook*, Vol. VI (November, 1956), pp. 4, 7, 24, and 25.

7. This statement is from a confidential interview on February 27, 1959.

8. See Reinhold Niebuhr, "A Note on Pluralism," *Religion in America*, John Cogley, ed. (Meridian Books, Inc., 1958), pp. 42–50.

9. See William W. Sweet, *The American Churches: An Interpretation* (Abingdon Press, 1948), Ch. I.

10. In the interest of fairness, an alternative interpretation of this practical expedient to meet a practical problem is stated by Leo Pfeffer, "The Case for Separation," *Religion in America*, pp. 52–94. The fact that by 1791 religious leaders among the Baptist, Presbyterian, Quakers, and Mennonites had turned down some fruits of establishment does not mean that the First Amendment was a matter of principle divorced from the objective fact of conflicting religious radicalism. Nor need we overlook the practicality of the First Amendment amid the lesser governments of the New World where religious interchange had been experienced. To the extent that this solution had become an option and the principle infused with value, it was seen as such by both religious statesmen and framers of the First Amendment.

See also Lloyd J. Averill, "In Defense of Christian Pluralism," *The Christian Century*, Vol. LXXVII, No. 22 (June 1, 1960), pp. 664–667.

11. For one of the better developments of the uniqueness and significance of this principle, see Leo Pfeffer, *Church, State, and Freedom* (The Beacon Press, Inc., 1953), Part I.

12. Thomas C. Hall, *The Religious Background of American Culture* (Little, Brown & Co., 1930); Pfeffer, *op. cit.*; Henry K. Rowe, *The History of Religion in the United States* (The Macmillan Company, 1924); William W. Sweet, *The Story of Religions in America* (Harper & Brothers, 1930); W. L. Sperry, *Religion in America* (Cambridge University Press, London, 1946).

13. Williams, *op. cit.*, pp. 318–319.

14. For a particularly good account, see William W. Sweet, "Cultural Pluralism in the American Tradition," *Christendom*, Vol. XI (Summer, 1946), pp. 316–326, and Vol. XII (Autumn, 1946), pp. 501–508.

15. To be sure, there is good reason for the religious institution to be concerned about going beyond efficiency, but this is beside the point in this discussion of the consequences of contemporary organizational structure. See Chapter VI where this problem is treated in a relevant context.

16. For a discussion of transition in organizational structure in the

delegation of responsibility through phases of administration to multiple organization, see Alvin Brown, *Organization: A Formulation of Principle* (Hibbert Printing Co., 1945).

17. Charles Clayton Morrison, *The Unfinished Reformation* (Harper & Brothers, 1953), p. 27.

18. *Ibid.*, p. 34.

19. Muelder, *loc. cit.*, p. 115.

20. Robert K. Merton, *Social Theory and Social Structure* (The Free Press of Glencoe, 1957), pp. 128–129, 421–436.

21. For a good survey of organizational fictions, see Robert Dubin, ed., *Human Relations in Administration: The Sociology of Organization* (Prentice-Hall, Inc., 1951), Ch. XX.

22. As used in this document, bureaucracy is not a pejorative epithet referring to inefficiency and red tape but a "type of organization designed to accomplish large-scale administrative tasks by systematically co-ordinating the work of many individuals."

23. Muelder, *loc. cit.*, p. 118.

24. Herberg, *op. cit.*, p. 280.

25. *Ibid.*, p. 64.

26. See Elmo Roper, "What People Are Thinking," *New York Herald Tribune* (July 3, 1947); NBC "Newsweek Documentaries" (December 27, 1953); and *Information Service* (April 3, 1954).

27. Herberg, *op. cit.*, pp. 64–65.

28. Stanley H. Chapman, "The Minister: Professional Man of the Church," *Social Forces,* Vol. XXIII (1944), p. 203.

29. Chester I. Barnard, "Functions of Status Systems in Formal Organizations," *Industry and Society,* W. F. Whyte, ed. (McGraw-Hill Book Company, Inc., 1946), pp. 48–49.

30. Lincoln Barnett, "God and the American People," *Ladies Home Journal* (November, 1948), p. 234.

31. "What the U.S. Thinks of Life Here and Hereafter," *The Catholic Digest* (May, 1933).

32. Barnett, *op. cit.*, pp. 233–235.

33. Herberg, *op. cit.*, pp. 85–86.

34. It might well be argued that a twenty to twenty-five-minute sermon on Sunday morning is not the place to deal with specific issues, and that it is the purpose of the sermon to motivate in the more general areas of Christian living. However, the occasional exception to the preaching pattern illustrates that this can be done effectively.

35. Samuel McCrea Cavert, *Yearbook of American Churches,* 1949, George F. Ketchum, ed. (National Council of the Churches of Christ in the U.S.A.), p. vi.

36. F. Ernest Johnson, "Neither Hot nor Cold," *Christianity and Crisis* (April 14, 1952), p. 41.

37. Albert Terrill Rasmussen, *Christian Social Ethics* (Prentice-Hall, Inc., 1956), p. 2.

38. Pope, *op. cit.*, p. 195.

39. Charles Y. Glock and Benjamin B. Ringer, "Church Policy and the

Attitudes of Ministers and Parishioners on Social Issues," *American Sociological Review*, Vol. XXI (April, 1956), pp. 148–156.

40. From a confidential interview on February 16, 1959.

41. Sheldon L. Messinger, "Organizational Transformation: A Case Study of a Declining Social Movement," *American Sociological Review*, Vol. XX (February, 1955), pp. 3–7.

42. Joseph Gusfield, "Social Structure and Moral Reform: A Study of the Woman's Christian Temperance Union," *American Journal of Sociology*, Vol. LXI (November, 1955), pp. 221–232.

43. See David Riesman, Nathan Glazer, and Reuel Denny, *The Lonely Crowd* (Yale University Press, 1950), p. 195.

44. Gusfield, *loc. cit.*, p. 232.

45. Russell R. Dynes, "Church-Sect Typology and Socioeconomic Status," *American Sociological Review*, Vol. XX (October, 1955), pp. 555–560. Used by permission.

46. Thomas Ford Hoult, "Economic Class Consciousness in American Protestantism," *American Sociological Review*, Vol. XV (February, 1950), pp. 97–100.

47. Statistics from *The San Francisco Bay Cities Baptist Union, Annual Report, 1957*, pp. 41, 42.

48. Statistics from the Presbyterian Church in the U.S.A., *Minutes of the General Assembly* of The United Presbyterian Church in the United States of America, Part III (1959), pp. 45–49.

49. See Melville Dalton, "Conflicts Between Staff and Line Managerial Officers," *American Sociological Review*, Vol. XV (June, 1950, pp. 342–351.

50. For a good discussion of line and staff tensions in a religious institution, see Robert Parks Rankin, "Religious Ideals and Church Administration: A Sociological Study of Methodism" (unpublished Ph.D. dissertation, Department of Sociology and Social Institutions, University of California, 1958).

51. This statement from confidential materials in a ministerial interview on February 25, 1959.

52. *Evangelism Through Teaching*, Leaflet N. 8321–B (General Board of Education, The Methodist Church).

53. *This We Can Do in Missionary and Stewardship Education* (Board of Education and Publication, American Baptist Convention), pp. 7, 8.

54. *Organizational Manual* (National Council of Presbyterian Men, Presbyterian Church in the U.S.A.), p. 36.

55. *The Schooner Club Manual* (unpublished manual drafted by First Presbyterian Church).

56. *With One Accord*, Leaflet N. 5M–10–58 (National Council of American Baptist Women, American Baptist Convention).

Chapter III. Social Selectivity in Adult Education

1. Wherever careful studies of church membership and participation have been made, religion has been found to reflect the general pattern of stratification in the community. Although precise details of definition and stratification vary from study to study, differences of class, status,

and power can be thought of as ranging on a continuum from low to high, and this continuum may be "sliced" into or analyzed into whatever number of social classes best meets the purposes of the analysis. For a bibliography of seventy-two entries on this topic, see that compiled by David O. Moberg in *Information Service*, Vol. XXXVII, No. 12 (June 14, 1958).

2. Walter Goldschmidt, "Class Denominationalism in Rural California Churches," *American Journal of Sociology*, Vol. XLIX (January, 1944), pp. 348–355.

3. Pope, *op. cit.*

4. Anton T. Boisen, *Religion in Crisis and Custom: A Sociological and Psychological Study* (Harper & Brothers, 1955).

5. H. Richard Niebuhr, *The Social Sources of Denominationalism.*

6. Walter Goldschmidt, *As You Sow* (The Free Press of Glencoe, 1947). Material used by permission. See also Goldschmidt, *loc. cit.*

7. *Ibid.,* p. 124.

8. *Ibid.,* pp. 133–134.

9. *Ibid.,* pp. 125–126.

10. *Ibid.,* p. 145.

11. *Ibid.*

12. *Ibid.,* p. 144.

13. Louis Bultena, "Church Membership and Church Attendance in Madison, Wisconsin," *American Sociological Review*, Vol. XIV (June, 1949), pp. 384–389.

14. Dynes, *loc. cit.,* p. 559.

15. *Ibid.* The author wishes to express his appreciation to Russell Dynes and the *American Sociological Review* for permission to utilize the Church-Sect scale in this research.

16. Pope, *op. cit.,* pp. 122–124. Liston Pope identified twenty-one indices in the movement from sect to church when a religious institution is "on the move." See also Earl D. C. Brewer, "Sect and Church in Methodism," *Social Forces*, Vol. XXV (May, 1952), pp. 400–408; S. D. Clark, *Church and Sect in Canada* (University of Toronto Press, Toronto, 1948), pp. 381–429; and Walter Muelder, "From Sect to Church," *Christendom*, Vol. XI (Autumn, 1945), pp. 450–462.

17. Dynes, *loc. cit.,* p. 559.

18. Geographical distance alone is not an adequate measurement of the universe of a parish. Certain psychological factors also come into play, such as the San Francisco Bay, which accents the geographical distance, and the freeways, which break down the barriers of distance.

19. The terms "nuclear," "modal," and "marginal" as used here do not imply that precise definitions have been utilized to characterize these rubrics. For a study based on such terms in a Roman Catholic church, see Joseph H. Fichter, *Social Relations in the Urban Parish* (University of Chicago Press, 1954).

20. As discussed below, these words appeared on the order of worship each Sunday while this study was made.

21. From a confidential interview on September 9, 1958.

22. From a confidential interview on September 10, 1958.

23. From a confidential interview on August 17, 1958.

24. From a confidential interview on August 26, 1958.

25. From an informal conversation on August 7, 1958.

26. From a confidential interview on September 25, 1958.

27. The term "ordinance" rather than "sacrament" is used in Baptist churches for what they prefer to call "the Lord's Supper" (rather than "Communion" or "Eucharist") and "Baptism." See A. Barclay, *The Protestant Doctrine of the Lord's Supper* (Robert MacLehose and Co., Ltd., Glasgow, 1928), Ch. II.

28. Kenneth Irving Brown, ". . . and Be Baptized": A Minister's Handbook on Baptism (The Judson Press, 1952).

29. From a confidential interview on October 17, 1958.

30. From a confidential interview on September 25, 1958.

31. From a confidential interview on September 26, 1958.

32. Interview on August 16, 1958.

33. From a confidential interview on September 22, 1958.

34. These three helpful terms are taken from the theoretical approach to small groups in George C. Homans, *The Human Group* (Harcourt, Brace and World, Inc., 1950).

35. A catering relationship of administration to clientele was also identified by Burton Clark, *op. cit.*, p. 85. However, the service character of adult education in the public schools has a much different set of restricting limitations as we shall see.

36. Robert Bales, *Interaction Process Analysis* (Addison-Wesley Publishing Company, 1950), Ch. III.

37. E. D. Chappel, "Measuring Human Relations: An Introduction to the Study of Interaction of Individuals," *Genetic Psychology Monographs*, Vol. XXII (1940), pp. 3–147.

38. W. F. Whyte, "Small Groups and Large Organizations," *Social Psychology at the Crossroads*, J. H. Rohrer and M. Sherif, eds. (Harper & Brothers, 1951).

39. Homans, *op. cit.*

40. C. M. Arensberg, "Behavior and Organization: Industrial Societies," *Social Psychology at the Crossroads*, Rohrer and Sherif, eds.

Chapter IV. The Role of the Bureaucratic Structure

1. *The Big Four Vital Questions About the Oakland Council of Churches.* This is an undated brochure published by the Oakland Council of Churches, Oakland, California.

2. From a confidential interview on March 5, 1959.

3. From an interview with the Director of the Protestant Social Welfare Bureau of the Oakland Council of Churches, March 5, 1959.

4. Northern California–Nevada Council of Churches, *The Church at Work*, Vol. XVII, No. 3 (March, 1959), p. 2.

5. Robert Michels, *Political Parties* (The Free Press of Glencoe, 1949), p. 373.

6. Minutes of the Annual Meeting, January 27, 1958, Oakland Council of Churches, Oakland, California. Used by permission.

7. For a more detailed analysis of the sources of income for local councils of churches, see the annual reports of the Office for Councils of Churches, National Council of the Churches of Christ in the U.S.A., 475 Riverside Drive, New York 27, N.Y.

8. For a more detailed analysis of the sources of income for state councils of churches, see the annual reports of the Office for Councils of Churches, National Council of the Churches of Christ in the U.S.A., 475 Riverside Drive, New York 27, N.Y.

9. Interview with Miss Margaret Lobb on May 5, 1959.

10. Statistics from Edward S. Setchko, "Toward an Informed Laity," *The Christian Century*, Vol. LXXVII (May 18, 1960), p. 603.

11. *Ibid.*

12. Among the centers of which this writer is aware are Parishfield, Michigan; Austin, Texas; Evanston, Illinois; Muskogee, Oklahoma; Lancaster, Pennsylvania; and Chicago, Illinois.

13. Although the faculty members of the Laymen's School have found that they have to teach these older, more experienced and frequently more secular-minded students differently from the way they teach theological students, many of them use the same texts as in their seminary classrooms, and a major paper is required for each six weeks.

14. Interview on May 31, 1960.

15. *Ibid.*

16. The Methodist Church, 9,670,690; The United Presbyterian Church in the U.S.A., 3,094,633; American Baptist Convention, 1,555,360. Statistics from Landis, *op. cit.*, pp. 253–258. Because of the merger of the Presbyterian Church in the U.S.A. and the United Presbyterian Church of North America, these figures were combined for The United Presbyterian Church in the U.S.A.

17. For a good description of the organization of The Methodist Church, see Nolan B. Harmon, *The Organization of The Methodist Church* (The Methodist Publishing House, 1953).

18. Costen J. Harrell, *The Local Church in Methodism* (The Methodist Publishing House, 1952), p. 14.

19. For a good description of Baptist polity, see William R. McNutt, *Polity and Practice in Baptist Churches* (The Judson Press, 1935).

20. Robert G. Torbet, *The Baptist Ministry Then and Now* (The Judson Press, 1953), pp. 9, 10.

21. For a description of Presbyterian polity, the following three books are useful: *The Constitution of The United Presbyterian Church in the United States of America* (The Office of the General Assembly of The United Presbyterian Church U.S.A.); *Presbyterian Law for the Local Church*, Eugene Carson Blake, ed. (The Office of the General Assembly of The United Presbyterian Church U.S.A.); *Presbyterian Law for the Presbytery*, Eugene Carson Blake and Edward Burns Shaw, eds. (The Office of the General Assembly of The United Presbyterian Church U.S.A.).

22. J. Aspinwall Hodge, *What Is Presbyterian Law?* (Presbyterian Board of Publications, 1882), pp. 11, 12.

23. Rankin, *op. cit.*, p. iv.

24. *A Manual on Ordination, Licensing, and Ministerial Listing* (The Judson Press). See also Torbet, *op. cit.*, pp. 123–133.

25. The problem of theological education among the Baptists has been discussed by Hugh Hartshorne and Milton C. Froyd, *Theological Education in the Northern Baptist Convention: A Survey, 1944–1945* (The Judson Press, 1945).

26. Confidential interview with an officer of the Northern California Baptist Convention, May 8, 1959.

27. Confidential interview with an officer of the American Baptist Union of the San Francisco Bay Cities, April 24, 1959.

28. For an account of the depreciation of episcopal powers in The Methodist Church, see Harmon, *op. cit.*, Part I.

29. See Rankin, *op. cit.*, for an especially good description of this phenomenon on higher organizational levels in the church.

30. For a discussion of the nature, causes, and effects of the "organizational revolution" and some case studies describing the impact upon different types of institutions, see Kenneth E. Boulding, *The Organizational Revolution: A Study in the Ethics of Economic Organizations* (Harper & Brothers, 1953).

31. Rankin, *op. cit.*, pp. 471–472.

Chapter V. Security and the Local Church

1. This was also the conclusion of Robert Parks Rankin, *op. cit.*, p. 225.

2. One of the characteristics of an old line institution is its ability to adapt to changing circumstances as a natural response to culture. Yet the questions "What shall we *be?*" and "What shall we *do?*" must constantly be asked by religious leaders to ascertain what "true commitments" an institution has which cannot change without damage to institutional integrity. A "liberal philosophy of group legitimacy" refers to one which is prepared to yield to societal pressures.

3. Although the term "infusion" signifies a purposeful activity calculated to introduce some element into the organization, it is not implied that this activity is consciously conceived and directed to offset needs and problems as rationally identified in this discussion. Rather, the infusion is a "natural" response to felt pressures (not necessarily identified as such) by religious leaders, and by the slow but continuous altering of leadership roles throughout an institutional history.

4. *Hillside Reminder* (mimeographed), November 3, 1959.

5. *Church Chatter* (mimeographed), May 28, 1959.

6. *Newssheet* (mimeographed), November, 1959.

7. From a group discussion at a meeting of the Men's Club, First Baptist Church, July 25, 1958.

8. *Temple Tidings*, April 12, 1959.

9. *Hillside Reminder* (mimeographed), October 1, 1959.

10. *Church Chatter* (mimeographed), October 14, 1959.

11. *The Book of Common Worship* (The United Presbyterian Church U.S.A., copyright, 1946, by the Board of Christian Education of the Presbyterian Church in the United States of America), p. 248.

12. The distinction between formal and informal structures is basic to the understanding of the institutional characteristics of the church. Too many persons have stopped characterizing the organizational structure of the church after describing the tasks and powers of its officers and the established system of rules. The end product is usually a constitution or an organizational chart. This only begins a story that might profitably have started elsewhere. A whole matrix of administrative characteristics and personal relationships, which no organizational chart or "officially approved pattern" can describe, emerges in every church. As these structures arise, they "fill in" and "influence" the formal structure, which has been defined by Broom and Selznick as "a system of rules and objectives defining the tasks, powers, and procedures of participants according to some officially approved pattern." For a good discussion of formal and informal structures, see Broom and Selznick, *op. cit.*, pp. 206–216.

13. *Ibid.*, pp. 213–216.

14. See Chapter II.

15. The "span of control" pertains to the extent to which an organization may direct the activities of its participants along desired lines. Since the connectional system in a local church is weak, the church must rely upon primary relations to provide a source of informal discipline, and socialization to provide a homogeneous social base. More will be said about these problems.

16. Broom and Selznick, *op. cit.*, pp. 124–126.

17. Charles Horton Cooley, *Social Organization* (Charles Scribner's Sons, 1909), Ch. III.

18. Broom and Selznick, *op. cit.*, p. 134.

19. From a confidential interview on September 4, 1958.

20. *The First Baptist Herald*, March 1, 1959.

21. Broom and Selznick, *op. cit.*, p. 216.

22. A phrase used by Herbert A. Simon, *Administrative Behavior* (The Macmillan Company, 1947), p. 103.

23. From a confidential interview on September 21, 1958.

24. John M. Mecklin, *The Passing of the Saint: A Study of a Cultural Type* (University of Chicago Press, 1941).

25. Selznick has described the use of insulation and absorption in gaining the total control of the individual in the combat parties of Bolshevic strategy. It is not uncommon for such extensive involvement in the Communist Party to effect a denial of the right of voluntary withdrawal. To leave the Party is not simply to dissociate oneself from a program, but is regarded as desertion in battle. See Philip Selznick, *The Organizational Weapon: A Study of Bolshevic Strategy and Tactics* (McGraw-Hill Book Company, Inc., 1952), pp. 25–29.

26. *Ibid.*

27. A mere organization is a technical instrument designed to accomplish definite goals. All phases of it are engineered to do a job and when that

job is accomplished and there is no further need for the organization, then it is expendable. Not so the church. It has been "institutionalized" through the acquiring of a self-distinctive identity—involving ways of acting and believing that are deemed important for their own sake. Although the institution is not expendable, there is a certain "lag" in the struggle to preserve the uniqueness in the face of new problems and altered circumstances. The "lag" (or conservatism) is characteristic of institutions that cannot be altered at will or eliminated entirely, as in the case of the technical organization.

Chapter VI. Administrative Involvement of the Minister

1. Selznick, *The Organizational Weapon,* p. 114. References to Selznick's study of Bolshevic strategy is not to assert that the church intentionally utilizes its indoctrination of clergymen as a diabolical means of maneuvering the masses as does communism. Doctrinal orthodoxies and institutional philosophies emerge in spontaneous and unplanned ways as unconscious aids to organizational security. Well-informed clergymen are a necessity in a contemporary society where secular doctrines constantly challenge teachings and behavior patterns of the religious community.

2. From observation of an "official board," March 24, 1959.

3. Paul M. Harrison has coined this term and identified this characteristic in the administration of the American Baptist Convention. See Paul M. Harrison, *Authority and Power in the Free Church Tradition* (Princeton University Press, 1959), pp. 189–190.

4. From a confidential interview on October 2, 1958.

5. For a good discussion of power, see Robert Bierstedt, "An Analysis of Social Power," *American Sociological Review,* Vol. XV (December, 1950), pp. 730–736.

6. Dubin, *op. cit.,* p. 172.

7. Harold D. Lasswell and Abraham Kaplan, *Power and Society* (Yale University Press, 1950), p. 133.

8. Simon, *op. cit.,* p. 125.

9. This term as used by Paul Harrison does not imply a formal apostolic succession, but it does denote a successor to the original charismatic founder (Jesus). Explains Harrison: "He is obeyed by the constituency because they believe he is endowed with sufficient qualities of the original leader to warrant obedience. . . . The expediential aspect of quasi-charismatic leadership is intensified by the fact that the latter-day leader must 'produce' in accord with the needs of the community, and with the established norms and ideals laid down in general terms by the charismatic founder." See Harrison, *op. cit.,* pp. 213–214.

10. *Ibid.,* Chs. IV and XI.

11. Max Weber, *The Theory of Social and Economic Organization,* tr. by A. M. Henderson and Talcott Parsons. (Oxford University Press, 1947), p. 328.

12. H. Richard Niebuhr, *The Purpose of the Church and Its Ministry* (Harper & Brothers, 1956), pp. vii–xvi.

13. Samuel W. Blizzard, "The Minister's Dilemma," *The Christian Century*, Vol. LXXV (April 25, 1956), p. 509.

14. *Ibid.*

15. *Ibid.*

16. David J. Ernsberger, *A Philosophy of Adult Christian Education* (The Westminster Press, 1959), p. 22.

17. *Ibid.*, pp. 22–23.

18. A rational method of administering a "smoothly running machine" places emphasis upon a neat, "logical" organization embodying efficient techniques of effecting uniformity and co-ordination. In answer to the question How can we make our organization more efficient? every task would be rationalized and the administration would insist that the resultant efficient procedures would be strictly followed. The thesis here is that in the local unit of the religious enterprises there are numerous irrationalities in the purely technical delineation of organizational tasks which give the local churches a distinctive character.

19. See p. 163

20. See pp. 84–90.

21. Landis, *op. cit.*, pp. 253–258.

22. Harrison, *op. cit.*, pp. 71–72.

23. Charles H. Page, "Bureaucracy and the Liberal Church," *Review of Religion*, Vol. XIV (March, 1952), pp. 141–142. Used by permission.

24. *Ibid.*, pp. 142–143.

25. Troeltsch, *op. cit.*, p. 331.

26. *Ibid.*, p. 336.

27. The role of the local clergyman is ambiguous in a variety of ways. He is a professionally trained man, yet he cannot utilize much of what he knows because of his lack of authority. He knows what has to be done in many situations, but he has to hunt around for indirect ways to influence others and win friends for his ideas. He is given little in the way of formal authority but must rely upon the establishment of informal mechanisms and "earned" power to motivate the leadership. He is a member of a community, yet he is in difficulty with its factions once he establishes friendships with particular groups. He has the mandate to preach prophetically, but he must not alienate the membership or restrict the flow of funds into the local and benevolent treasuries. Such are the ambiguities in the "no man's land" where the local clergyman must "walk on eggs" to administrate his local church.

28. Definition from Broom and Selznick, *op. cit.*, p. 238.

Chapter VII. The Mission of Adult Education

1. This quip is one of the well-turned phrases of Martin E. Marty, *The New Shape of American Religion*, p. 131.

2. F. W. Dillistone, *The Structure of the Divine Society* (The Westminster Press, 1951).

3. Suzanne de Dietrich, *The Witnessing Community: The Biblical Record of God's Purpose* (The Westminster Press, 1958).

4. Howard Grimes, *The Church Redemptive* (Abingdon Press, 1958).

5. Minear, *op. cit.*

6. Robert McAfee Brown, *The Significance of the Church* (The Westminster Press, 1956).

7. Emil Brunner, *The Misunderstanding of the Church*, tr. by Harold Knight (The Westminster Press, 1953).

8. H. Richard Niebuhr, *The Purpose of the Church and Its Ministry.*

9. R. Newton Flew, ed., *The Nature of the Church: Papers Presented to the Theological Commission Appointed by the Continuation Committee of the World Conference on Faith and Order* (Harper & Brothers, 1951).

10. Selznick, *Leadership in Administration*, p. 66.

11. Report of the Advisory Commission on the Main Theme of the Second Assembly of the World Council of Churches, "Christ—the Hope of the World," *The Christian Hope and the Task of the Church* (Harper & Brothers, 1954), p. 1.

12. *Ibid.*, p. 14.

13. C. L. Patijn, "The Strategy of the Church," The Church and the Disorder of Society, Vol. III of *Man's Disorder and God's Design* (Harper & Brothers, 1948), p. 155.

14. Although these councils do not determine the official theological and doctrinal position of the churches involved in the discussions, they do represent a high degree of consensus on the part of the respected denominational leaders upon the "burning concerns of all the churches in this crisis of civilization."

15. H. Richard Niebuhr, *The Purpose of the Church and Its Ministry*, p. 18.

16. Paul Vieth, "What Is Happening in Christian Education?" *Yale Divinity News* (January, 1959).

17. James D. Smart, *The Teaching Ministry of the Church* (The Westminster Press, 1954).

18. Lewis Joseph Sherrill, *The Gift of Power* (The Macmillan Company, 1955).

19. Randolph Crump Miller, *Biblical Theology and Christian Education* (Charles Scribner's Sons, 1956).

20. Grimes, *op. cit.*

21. Reuel Howe, *Man s Need and God's Action* (The Seabury Press, Inc., 1953).

22. Miller, *op. cit.*, p. 191.

23. From confidential materials.

24. For an account of the neglect of theologians to study the institutional factors related to unity and disunity in the ecumenical movement, see the address by Dean Walter G. Muelder, "Institutionalism in Relation to Unity and Disunity," *The Nature of the Unity We Seek*, pp. 90–102.

25. The term "situation-conditioned" is taken from the paper of George Florovsky entitled "The Church: Her Nature and Task." See George Florovsky, in *Man's Disorder and God's Design* (Harper & Brothers, 1948), Vol. II, pp. 43–44.

26. H. Richard Niebuhr, *The Purpose of the Church and Its Ministry*, p. 90.

27. *Ibid.*, pp. 79 f.

28. Samuel W. Blizzard, "The Minister's Dilemma," *The Christian Century*, Vol. LXXIII (April 25, 1956), p. 510.

29. H. Richard Niebuhr, *The Purpose of the Church and Its Ministry*, pp. 83–84.

30. Chester Barnard uses this phrase in another connection, cf. *The Function of the Executive* (Harvard University Press, 1938), p. 168.

31. Harrison, *op. cit.*, pp. 148–149.

32. Brunner, *op. cit.*, p. 17.

33. *Ibid.*, p. 109.

34. Grimes, *op. cit.*, p. 160.

35. This theme is best handled by Philip Selznick, *Leadership in Administration*, who declares that "the executive becomes a statesman as he makes the transition from administrative management to institutional leadership."

36. H. Richard Niebuhr, *The Purpose of the Church and Its Ministry*, p. 39.

37. Selznick, *Leadership in Administration*, p. 119.

38. *Ibid.*, pp. 138–139.

39. Eph. 4:11–12.

40. A sample statement of such dissatisfaction is included in a pamphlet published by the Board of Christian Education of The United Presbyterian Church in the U.S.A.: "It is curious that the earliest, simple Bible teachings that we impart to children—for example, 'love one another'—are devoted so frequently to the ethical injunctions that are conspicuously not obeyed in the average church. We have created an elaborate apparatus in our Sunday church school organization to teach the young those very things they may never experience in church life. There is more than irony in this situation. There is the signficant fact that we have delegated to certain individuals and organizations the task of delivering a message that ought to be voiced and exemplified by everyone within the church. In other words, we have delegated what *cannot* be passed off as somebody else's responsibility; and so we nullify the teachings that we expect somebody else to teach. If 'love one another' is a valid commandment for Christian life together, then it cannot simply be left in the hands of professional or semiprofessional workers whose job it is to make such a teaching meaningful." See *Parents Are Teachers Too* (Board of Christian Education of The United Presbyterian Church in the U.S.A., 1956), p. 12.

41. Smart, *op. cit.*, p. 11.

42. Ernsberger, *op. cit.*, pp. 45–46.

43. C. H. Dodd, *Apostolic Preaching and Its Developments* (Willett, Clark & Company, 1937), p. 3.

44. Smart, *op. cit.*, pp. 19–20.

45. Grimes, *op. cit.*, p. 105.

46. Vieth, *loc. cit.*

47. Ernsberger, *op. cit.*, p. 56.

48. Such an argument comes from Robert Lee, *The Social Sources of Church Unity.*

49. Burton Clark, *op. cit.*, p. 149.

50. This wording is taken from the defined task of The Fund for Adult Education of the Ford Foundation. See *Continuing Liberal Education,* a report of The Fund for Adult Education 1957–1959, White Plains, New York.